THE DECLINE OF TRADE UNION ORGANISATION

The level of trade union membership in Britain is at its lowest point since the late 1960s and is continuing to decline. Optimists argue that this decline is the result mainly of growing unemployment and that it will be made good as full employment returns. This book considers the reasons for the decline and discusses the prospects for recovery. It shows that many factors are at work besides unemployment growth and overall it argues that the changing structure and nature of British industry is having a fundamental affect on the nature of trade union activity. It points to recent legislation which protects individual employees without the need for union involvement; to the fact that a major growth area is the private services sector which has been poorly unionised traditionally; and to the fact that much industrial growth is occurring in smaller plants (again poorly unionised traditionally) and in areas of the country where trade unionism does not have the same strong tradition as in the older manufacturing areas. It charts the changing attitude of management towards unions, arguing that anti-union attitudes are growing in sophistication and confidence. It discusses the increase in non-union plants, particularly amongst American multinationals' subsidiaries, and relates this to the major concessions made by some unions by making no-strike agreements and so on. It also discusses the situation in the public sector and makes comparisons with the USA, where the decline of union membership has been much more spectacular and fundamental.

P.B. Beaumont, Reader in Industrial Relations, University of Glasgow

D1345079

THE DECLINE OF TRADE UNION ORGANISATION

P.B. BEAUMONT

CROOM HELM
London • Sydney • Wolfeboro, New Hampshire

© 1987 P.B. Beaumont
Croom Helm Ltd, Provident House, Burrell Row,
Beckenham, Kent, BR3 1AT
Croom Helm Australia, 44-50 Waterloo Road,
North Ryde, 2113, New South Wales

British Library Cataloguing in Publication Data

Beaumont, P.B.
    The decline of trade union organisation
    1. Trade unions — Great Britain —
    History — 20th century
    I. Title
    331.88′0941   HD6664
    ISBN 0-7099-3958-2

Croom Helm US, 27 South Main Street,
Wolfeboro, New Hampshire 03894-2069

Library of Congress Cataloging-in-Publication Data

Beaumont, P.B. (Phil B.)
    The decline of trade union organization.

    Includes index.
    1. Trade-unions — Great Britain. 2. Industrial
relations — Great Britain. I. Title.
HD6664.B355 1987   331.88′0941   86-16234
ISBN 0-7099-3958-2 (U.S.)

Printed and bound in Great Britain
by Billing & Sons Limited, Worcester.

CONTENTS

TO PAT

A SUMMARY STATEMENT

The starting point for this book is the substantial fall in union density that has occurred in the
UK since 1979.   The factors behind this decline
are viewed as transcending the current economic
recession, with a management reaction against the
institution of unionism at the organisational level
being a major potential influence examined.   The
book seeks to identify the various incentives and
enabling conditions that would be involved in such
a reaction, with particular attention being paid to
the various ways in which this reaction could
manifest itself through the course of time.
Despite the fact that union density only peaked in
the UK some six years ago, there are already some
early signs of such a reaction, although whether
this is the beginning of a process of decline
similar to that which has occurred in the United
States seems rather more doubtful in view of certain
significant differences between the two systems of
industrial relations.   These different enabling
conditions at the present time should not, however,
obscure the fact that similar incentives for such
a move exist in both systems.

LIST OF TABLES:

List of Tables

GLOSSARY

ACTWU	Amalgamated Clothing and Textile Workers Union
AFL-CIO	American Federation of Labor - Congress of Industrial Organizations
AMPS	Association of Managerial and Professional Staff
APEX	Association of Professional, Executive, Clerical and Computer Staffs
ASLEF	Associated Society of Locomotive Engineers and Firemen
ASTMS	Association of Scientific, Technical and Managerial Staffs
AUEW	Amalgamated Union of Engineering Workers
AUEW-TASS	Amalgamated Union of Engineering Workers - Technical, Administrative and Supervisory Section
BIFU(NUBE)	Banking, Insurance and Finance Union (formerly National Union of Bank Employees)
COHSE	Confederation of Health Service Employees
CPSA	Civil and Public Services Association
EETPU	Electric, Electronics, Telecommunications and Plumbing Union
EAT	Employment Appeal Tribunal
EMA	Engineers and Managers Association
FBU	Fire Brigades Union
GMWU	General and Municipal Workers Union
ISTC	Iron and Steel Trades Federation
NALGO	National and Local Government Officers Association
NAS/UWT	National Association of Schoolmasters and Union of Women Teachers
NUM	National Union of Mineworkers
NUPE	National Union of Public Employees
NUR	National Union of Railwaymen

Glossary

NUT	National Union of Teachers
POEU	Post Office Engineering Union
RCN	Royal College of Nursing
SCPS	Society of Civil and Public Servants
TGWU	Transport and General Workers Union
TSSA	Transport Staffs Salaried Association
UAW	United Automobile Workers
UCW	Union of Communication Workers

ACKNOWLEDGEMENTS

There are numerous people who provided information,
assistance and advice which greatly assisted me
in the preparation of this book.   In this regard
special mention should be made of the numerous
discussions with Andrew Thomson that encouraged
me to think about producing a book along these
lines.   I am also grateful to officers of ACAS in
Scotland, the Northern Ireland Labour Relations
Agency, the Labour Research Department and Incomes
Data Services for providing access to various
sources of information.   The work done with a
number of researchers at other institutions, as
well as with various graduate students at Glasgow,
made a significant contribution to the final
product, while the discussions with, and illustrative material provided by, a number of union and
management individuals was most helpful.   Maureen
Robb provided her usual invaluable research
assistance, while Mary Steventon dealt efficiently
and humorously with more drafts of individual
chapters than she and I could, or would want to,
remember.

Chapter One

SETTING THE SCENE

There have been a number of recent predictions
regarding the future position and role of trade
unions in the United Kingdom.   For example,
Michael Rose has suggested that trade unions face
the prospect of becoming increasingly inconsequen-
tial in the future employment environment unless
they can take a lead in generating '... original
but practical ideas for restructuring work and
employment patterns, in a framework other than
that imposed by ad hoc bargaining or by techno-
cratic logic'.(1)   And Charles Handy has predicted
that the collective bargaining function of trade
unions will increasingly decline as a result of
important changes in the nature of industrial
organisations.(2)   The particular changes mentioned
being organisations increasingly characterised by
relatively small plant size, geographical diversity,
federal and contractual based structures.
According to Handy the future for trade unions lies
in increasingly adopting an advisory-advocacy role
for individual employees a la the guild model,
although there are, in his view, few signs that the
unions have accepted this fact.
      These sorts of predictions have obviously been
strongly influenced by what has occurred to the
trade union movement in the high unemployment years
since 1979, a period of time that has also seen an
extremely right wing Conservative administration
in office.   The most obvious indication of the
changed fortunes of the trade union movement in
the United Kingdom since 1979 is that set out
in Table 1.1.
      The picture revealed by Table 1.1 is that of
relative stability in union density in the 1960s,
substantial growth in the 1970s and sizeable decline
in the years since 1979.   In considering the

1

Table 1.1:   Union Density of the Workforce
              in the UK, 1960-1984

Year	Percentage Unionised
1960	44.2
1961	44.0
1962	43.8
1963	43.7
1964	44.1
1965	44.2
1966	43.6
1967	43.6
1968	44.0
1969	45.3
1970	48.5
1971	48.7
1972	49.5
1973	49.3
1974	50.4
1975	51.0
1976	51.9
1977	53.4
1978	54.2
1979	55.4
1980	53.6
1981	51.0
1982	48.2
1983	45.5
1984	45.0

Source: A. Oswald and P. Turnbull, 'Pay and
Employment Determination in Britain: What are
Labour Contracts Really Like?', Centre for Labour
Economics, LSE, Discussion Paper No. 212, February
1985.

figures in Table 1.1 one needs to be mindful of the
basis on which they are compiled.   A recent paper
by Walsh, for example, discusses the problem of
compiling such a series, using the membership
records of individual trade unions.(3)   Walsh
particularly stresses the potential importance of
trying to identify the 'active' component of
membership, that is those union members paying
full dues who are in employment.   In the post
1979 years the lack of success of the trade unions
in retaining membership among the unemployed has
been highlighted.(4)   This retention problem in a
setting of high unemployment disproportionately
concentrated on the relatively unionised parts of
the economy (i.e. the manufacturing sector and

within it industries like engineering) means that
there will have been a fall in total union membership, and a fall in union density when the total
workforce includes the unemployed.   However,
given the 'active' membership stress of Walsh one
might want to   argue that the figures in Table 1.1
rather exaggerate the extent of the difficulties
faced by unions in terms of their effective day to
day dealings with management if they have maintained union density among the employed section
of the workforce.   The existence of closed shop
and check off arrangements could be viewed as
having assisted such an outcome.   Although no
direct test of this is possible, excluding the
unemployed from the workforce total produces the
following union density figures:

1979	58.1
1980	58.2
1981	56.3
1982	53.9
1983	53.1

The above figures indicate that the fall in
union density is only about half of that when the
unemployed are included in the workforce total.
There are two other comments on the figures in
Table 1.1 which are worthy of some note.   The
first is that the increased union density of the
1970s has been viewed by at least one commentator
as essentially 'paper growth' involving little in
the way of a development or reflection of genuine
trade union consciousness;(5)   the implication
here would seem to be that such growth was basically fragile, and as such could be relatively
easily reversed.   Secondly, these figures have
been utilised in a variety of studies, particularly those concerned with inflation, as the index
of union power.   In fact it is extremely
difficult to adequately represent the complex,
multi-dimensional notion of 'union power' by any
single index or measure.   These figures are
certainly not intended for such a purpose here,
although it is hard to believe that many commentators would disagree with the proposition that a
substantial fall in union density is unlikely to
be associated with a situation of generally
rising union power.   The concentration on union
density here derives from its value as a useful
concept for organising material around in order
to illustrate the changing features and facets of

the industrial relations system.

To some commentators the decline in union density since 1979 is understandable, predictable, and, perhaps for these reasons, not all that worrying. This sort of view starts from the position that historically trade union membership and density has always tended to fall in high unemployment years. Moreover, it is often argued that trade unions have been the benefici- aries of 'social disasters' in that union density has increased significantly in war-time periods, and has often increased substantially in the up- swing of the business cycle immediately following a deep depression or recession. The latter effect has been attributed to an increase in the stock of worker grievances in the depression years when management has tended to treat individual employees 'harshly' or 'carelessly'. This rather 'cavalier' treatment by management is held to produce a latent demand for unionism which becomes realised when relative economic prosperity returns. As an accompaniment to this argument, one might also want to suggest that the current recession will increase the number, and possibly the 'quality' of mergers among unions (the number of trade unions in the UK has fallen from 565 in 1969 to 401 in 1982) with the result that a much 'leaner' and more 'efficient' trade union movement will emerge.

To argue, however, that trade union member- ship and density will 'bounce back' in a similar fashion (to the past) when the present recession ends is to assume, firstly, that management will currently make the same 'treatment of employee' mistakes that they made in, for example, the 1930s. And, secondly, it assumes that the extent and nature of the economic upturn following the present recession will be essentially similar to that which has occurred previously. Both assump- tions may be, and indeed have been, questioned. For example, the likelihood that the upturn will be more an output than an employment one, the availability of 'new technology' (with its poten- tially adverse employment implications) in a wide variety of industries, and the adoption of a 'sophisticated paternalistic style' of management in those parts of the economy where unionism is not well entrenched have all been cited as factors limiting the likelihood of history repeating itself in this regard.(6) Most importantly of

all is the question of whether the forces working
to lower overall union density in the UK are
essentially recession-related forces. The contention here is that the extent of trade union
organisation in the future in the UK is being
shaped by factors that transcend the current
economic recession. The nature of these adverse
factors can be usefully illustrated by considering
the high union growth years of the 1970s where
they were apparent even then.

The Growth Years, 1969-1979

In the ten years 1969-1979 trade union density in
the UK increased by some 10 percentage points,
reaching an all-time peak of 55 per cent of the
workforce in 1979; this figure was some 10 percentage points above the previous peak years of
1920 and 1948.(7) These years were, together
with those of 1911-1920 and 1934-1948, the most
dramatic growth years for unions in the UK, with
the extent of the gains in 1969-1979 being impressive even by international standards.(8) This
growth was, however, overwhelmingly concentrated
in the already well unionised parts of the economy,
namely manufacturing and the public sector where
some 85 per cent of the membership increase
occurred. The figures produced by Price and Bain
for union density in the different sectors of the
economy in 1979 were as follows:

Public sector	82.4
Manufacturing	69.8
Construction	36.7
Agriculture, forestry and fishing	22.7
Private services	16.7

The first potential problem for the trade
union movement suggested here is the possibility
of a saturation effect, particularly in the case
of the public sector. The point here is simply
that the public sector was so highly unionised by
1979 that there would appear to be relatively
little scope for a further increase in union
density of any substantial size and/or which could
be obtained without a disproportionate investment
of effort and resources.

A second problem for the unions is indicated
by the relatively low union density figure for
private sector services in 1979. Admittedly,
union membership in private sector services
increased by some 60 per cent in the years 1969-

5

1979, but union density only rose by some 4 percentage points in that time, a level only 2 percentage points higher than that in 1948.   In 1979 the poorly unionised sectors, such as private sector services, accounted for approximately 40 per cent of potential union membership, but only 15 per cent of actual membership.   The poor historical record of the unions in achieving recognition in private sector services is typically attributed to a conjunction of factors, most notably small establishment size, part-time working, high labour turnover and strongly entrenched employer opposition.   Moreover, the relative expansion of private sector services in employment terms poses a problem for the future maintenance of overall workforce union density;   the Institute of Employment Research, for example, has estimated that nearly two-thirds of all the net new jobs in Britain in 1985-1990 will be in private sector services.(9)   According to Price and Bain's estimates overall union density would still be some 4 percentage points lower in 1990 than it was in 1979, even if the unions managed to maintain throughout the 1980s (which they clearly have not done to date) the levels of union density achieved in all sectors in 1979.   This 'silent thief' effect is attributable to the relative increase of women workers, white collar workers and changes in the industrial composition of the workforce as a whole.

The fact that the direction of change in the occupational and industrial distribution of the workforce is working against the overall maintenance of union density in the UK is well known.   This is frequently viewed in terms of an inter-industry process of change with the general direction of movement being from the manufacturing sector to the services sector.   However, important occupational changes can occur within individual industries, and indeed within individual organisations.   It is now well recognised that the organisation of large corporations has typically involved the creation of a number of divisions each subdivided further into wholly owned limited liability companies which may in turn have a number of establishments.   And the dominance of these multi-divisional (or M-form) corporations appears to have increased in the manufacturing sector in recent decades.   For example, the number of enterprises with 10,000 or more employees (i.e. 74 in 1958 and 83 in 1978)

which owned, on average, 30 establishments in 1958
(and 40 in 1978) accounted for 25% of the manufacturing workforce in 1958 and 33% in 1978.(10)
     The point here is that the level of union
density is likely to vary quite considerably
between the divisions, companies and individual
establishments of these major corporations.   And
if any restructuring that takes place is disproportionately concentrated in the more highly unionised
parts of the corporation the result will be a
reduction in the overall union density of the
corporation which, in turn, will lower the overall
density of any industry in which it is a major
employer.   This sort of effect was certainly
observable in the example cited below.
     In 1977 this particular corporation was
divided into 4 divisions and comprised 14 separate
companies.   By 1985 there were 16 separate
companies, but spread over only 3 divisions.   In
1977 the corporation had over 20,000 employees with
overall union density being some 65%.   There was,
however, considerable variation in the level of
union density within the corporation.   For example,
union density among staff was 27%, whereas among
the shop floor employees it averaged 80%.   There
was also notable variation between the different
divisions (and individual companies) of the corporation;   for example, union density among staff in
the separate divisions in 1977 was 51%, 37%, 29%
and 17%.
     In the period 1977-1985 total employment in
the corporation fell by some 46% while the overall
level of union density fell by approximately 13%
(i.e. 65% to 52%) for the corporation as a whole.
In seeking to account for the latter the first
point to note is that the employment reduction
disproportionately affected the shop floor grades.
Their employment fall was some 55% compared to only
23% for staff.   As a result, the proportion of
total employment in the corporation accounted for
by the staff grades rose from 27% in 1977 to 39%
in 1985;   this obviously acted to lower overall
union density given that union density among staff
was only 27% compared to 80% for the shopfloor in
1977.   Secondly, we found that the union membership fall among staff in the period 1977-1985 was
fully 53% compared to an employment fall of only
23%;   for the shopfloor there was little difference
between the fall in union membership (57%) and the
fall in employment (55%).   This dramatic fall in
staff union membership and density (from 27%

in 1977 to 17% in 1985) was largely due to the fact
that employment reductions among staff in 1977-
1985 were disproportionately concentrated among the
lower grades which were the more highly unionised
of the staff grades.   As a result, the more senior
grades of staff, which had little in the way of
union representation in 1977, have become a higher
proportion of the total number of staff in the
period 1977-1985, but with no commensurate increase
in their level of union organisation over this
time.

In summary, this particular corporation's
restructuring process has involved a significant
change in the composition of its workforce with a
shift towards (i) staff grades relative to shop
floor workers and (ii) senior grades relative to
the lower grades of staff.   The not inconsiderable
existence of post entry closed shop arrangements
have acted to very largely maintain union density
among the shopfloor (80% in 1977 and 76% in 1985),
but this maintenance effect has been over-ridden
by the effect of the above two changes, with the
result being a quite considerable decline in
overall union density for the corporation in this
eight-year period.

Another potential problem area for the trade
union movement is suggested by the contents of
Table 1.2 below.

The figures in Table 1.2 indicate that
employment growth in the manufacturing sector is
being increasingly based in small towns and rural
areas.   The work of Massey and Miles has explicitly
considered the causes and implications of the
geographical dispersion of trade union membership
which has been going on over the last 20 years.(11)
To illustrate the extent of change in this regard
consider the case of the Amalgamated Union of
Engineering Workers which in 1951 had some three
and a half thousand more members in its historic
base areas (i.e. London, Lancashire, Birmingham/
Coventry, South Wales, Glasgow/Paisley) than in
the rest of the country.   But by 1979 these
'heartland' areas had some 120,000 fewer members
than the rest of the country.   This sort of spatial
dispersion effect is seen to be the result of the
secular decline of older industries, changes in
production technology and the increased tendency of
firms to locate in smaller sized towns;   the latter
decisions are seen to be motivated, at least in
substantial part, by a desire to obtain a less
well organised and more compliant workforce (in

Table 1.2:   Manufacturing Employment by
              Type of Area, 1960-1978

	Employment (000s)		% Change 1960-78
	1960	1978	
London	1,338	768	-42.5
Conurbations	2,282	1,677	-26.5
Free standing cities	1,331		-13.8
Large towns	921	901	- 2.2
Small towns	1,631	1,887	+15.7
Rural areas	527	728	+38.0
Great Britain	8,031	7,110	-11.5

Conurbations:	Manchester, Merseyside, Clydeside, Tyneside, West Yorkshire, West Midlands.
Free standing cities:	Other cities with more than 250,000 people.
Large towns:	Towns or cities with between 100,000 and 250,000 people.
Small towns:	Local authority districts including at least one settlement with between 35,000 and 100,000 people.
Rural areas:	Local authority districts in which all settlements have less than 35,000 people.

Source: Charles Handy, The Future of Work, Basil
Blackwell, Oxford, 1984, p.85.

---

fact this is more an assertion than an empirically
established relationship).   This increased decentralisation of industry and trade union membership leads to increased competition for the jobs
of mobile industry between different areas and
hence between different parts of the trade union
movement.   One result that Massey and Miles
attribute to this change is the increased incidence
of single union recognition agreements very much
on management's terms.   They also argue that the
result is now a much greater capacity to operate
on a non-union basis in the UK.   These two results
are most apparent in the new, high technology
industries where, for example, a recent Labour
Research Department study noted that 19 of the 33
major information technology producing companies

9

in the country are non-union, and that even   '...
where there has been unionisation ... it has often
been on terms very different from traditional practices with controversial no-strike clauses...'(12)

These sorts of structural changes are not the
only ones that raise difficulties for the unions
seeking to maintain, much less increase, the
proportion of the workforce that is organised in
the UK in the future.   The following section
contains a list of some of the other potential
problem areas that have increasingly suggested
themselves from the 1970s.

A Check List of Possible Problem Areas
for the Unions

The first possible candidate is the passage of
legislation giving rights to individual employees,
as opposed to trade union members.   The particular
fear here, which is historically associated with
the 'business union' views of Samuel Gompers in the
United States, is that such legislation will
detract from (i.e. substitute for) rather than add
to (i.e. complement) the level of employee demand
for the job protective services of unions.   In
the UK the most obvious example of such legislation
is that concerned with unfair dismissal.   And
certainly the available evidence indicates that
individuals claiming unfair dismissal are disproportionately likely to have been employed in
small, non-union establishments.   There is, for
example, a consistent, negative (if not always
significant) correlation between the extent of
unfair dismissal applications and collective
bargaining coverage at the industry level in the
years 1974-1976.   Secondly, Employers Protection
Insurance Services, which has since 1976 offered
firms insurance protection against appearing before
an industrial tribunal, cites as its typical
customer an establishment of less than 200 employees
that is not unionised.(13)   And more recently a
survey of over 1,000 unfair dismissal claimants
reported that only some 32 per cent of them were
union members.(14)   The TUC appear to have taken
a rather sanguine view of this situation, having
gone on record in the following terms: 'The General
Council value the work done by industrial tribunals
in providing a measure of protection to workpeople,
particularly where it has not been possible to
develop effective union organisation.   Disproportionate numbers of complaints against unfair

dismissal come from weakly organised occupations or sectors, or from non-union small firms, and industrial tribunals have shown themselves to be the only effective protection for these workers.' (15)   However, if this sort of pattern remains among unfair dismissal applicants over an extended period of time the trade unions might increasingly come to view the decision to retain the unfair dismissal provisions of the Industrial Relations Act 1971 as being a far from costless one to them.

Historically, trade union recognition, particularly among white collar grades of employees, has been associated with Government pressure to this end being exerted through the medium of Employers Associations.(16)   This has been most obvious during the two wartime periods.(17) However, with the UK now, at least in the private sector, being very much a system of single employer bargaining at the plant and, to a lesser extent, the company level the capacity of any Government to act in this way is very much reduced.   This important departure from the European model of highly centralised bargaining structures, with a resulting reduction in the power and authority of individual employers associations, would seem to enhance the ability of firms wishing to operate on a non-union basis in the UK.   These two changes obviously have a very UK-specific element about them.   In contrast, the two areas of change to be discussed now have been most emphasised in the US context, although as we hope to demonstrate their potential for lowering the level of union density is likely to transcend any one national system of industrial relations.

Increased Competition and New Organisational Arrangements

In fact the first potential area of change to be discussed here was suggested by the earlier quoted view of Handy.   The view there was that fundamental changes in the economic environment are necessitating significant changes in the strategy, culture, structure and working arrangements of organisations. Piore and Sabel, for example, have argued that the general increase in competitive pressures and the movement away from the production of relatively standardised products (due to factors such as the availability of new computer-based technologies that reduce the costs of flexible production techniques) are leading to more flexible forms of

work organisation.(18)   The general direction of
organisational change appears to be towards, what
Handy terms, a 'task culture', which is held to be
the most adaptive structure in an environment of
competition and relatively short product life
cycles.(19)   One particular view of this 'new
organisational form' is that set out in Table 1.3;
there are, of course, many similar listings, most
notably those of Lawler and Walton in the United
States.

These new flexible forms of work organisation
and practice are held to be very much associated
with non-union 'greenfield site' establishments in
the United States; a recent conference board
study, for example, reported that firms in which
there had been a significant fall in union membership between 1977 and 1983 were, among other things,
characterised by the opening of new plants and the
introduction of workplace innovations in non-union
facilities.(20)   In the UK there has been considerable discussion, at least in the popular
management literature, of greenfield site operations.   A recent study of four such sites identified the following common features of work organisation there: (21)

(i)   fewer tiers of management;
(ii)   abolition of the roles of chargehands, fore-
        men and conventional supervisors, with
        enhanced status of first line managers;
(iii)   minimisation of status differences;
(iv)   giving groups of employees joint responsi-
        bility for a range of tasks;
(v)   dissemination of more information on work-
        related matters;
(vi)   communication to and from employees directly,
        through group meetings rather than through
        trade unions.

The UK greenfield site literature, in contrast
to that of the United States, does not have an
explicit non-union dimension; in fact 3 out of the
4 case studies above were unionised establishments.
Moreover, greenfield site establishments with the
above features probably constitute a very small
proportion of existing establishments in the UK,
if only because the current recession appears to
have put a considerable brake on the process of
organisation growth through the building of new
plants.   Nevertheless, the introduction of
flexible working arrangements of this sort, _if_

Table 1.3:   Features of Traditional and
             New Organisations

Traditional	New
The technological imperative	Joint optimisation
Man as an extension of the machine	Man as complementary to the machine
An expendable spare part	A resource to be developed
Maximum task breakdown, single narrow skills	Optimum task grouping, multiple broad skills
External controls (supervisors, specialist staffs, procedures)	Internal controls (self regulating sub-systems)
Tall organisational chart, autocratic style	Flat organisational chart, participative style
Competition, gamesmanship	Collaboration, collegiality
Organisation's purposes only	Members and society's purposes also
Alienation	Commitment
Low risk taking	Innovation

Source: Michael Cross, 'Flexibility and
Integration at the Workplace', Employee Relations,
Vol. 7, No. 1, 1985, p.4.

disproportionately concentrated in the lesser
unionised parts of multi-establishment organisations
(e.g. the plants outside the large metropolitan
centres) could limit the future level of employee
demand for unionisation in such organisations.
This is because of the potential of such flexible
working arrangements to produce a strong employee-
organisation identification process that limits
the emergence of the job dissatisfaction that is
held to be an essential prerequisite for employees
demanding unionisation.   And if their effect is to
limit the achievement of union recognition in the
relatively expanding parts of an individual
organisation the result will be a fall in the
overall level of union density for the organisation;   the larger behavioural implications of

flexible working arrangements are obviously
extremely important in unionised work settings,
but are outwith the discussion here, given our
focus solely on union density.

In the United States the introduction of
flexible working arrangements has been held to be
fundamentally stimulated by changes in technology
and product market conditions, rather than by a
simple union avoidance motive. The recent survey
by Edwards of senior management in some 220 UK
establishments certainly indicated the considerable
introduction of flexible working arrangements
(and new technology) in response to increased
competitive pressures;(22) some 84% of the
respondents reported increased competition over the
previous 3 years, while 74% stated that they
faced strong or very strong competition from abroad.
In addition to such survey responses there are
objective indications of the increased competitive
pressures facing UK management. Michael Chisholm,
for example, recently argued that:(23)

> A considerable amount of work has been done in
> attempts to measure competitiveness, in terms
> especially of market shares, unit costs and
> the embodiment of new technology. However,
> the only measure of overall competitiveness
> which takes account of all factors is actual
> performance in export markets relative to the
> success of other nations in exporting in the
> country in question, in this case the United
> Kingdom. Therefore, the examination of
> import and export performance is the single
> most useful approach.

Chisholm then went on to produce the figures
set out in Table 1.4 below, which indicate considerable inter-industry variation in the extent
of change in the Import/Export ratio for these
years; the largest adverse change was in vehicles,
with the most favourable change being for timber
and furniture manufacturing. However, fully 12
of the 17 industry orders had adverse changes in
the period 1971-1982. The most severe losses of
employment were generally associated with industries
experiencing the most adverse changes in this
measure of competitiveness, although the relationships with productivity change and that in output
were rather less systematic.

In addition to this environmental change one also needs to consider the possibility that the extent and nature of management opposition to (or, conversely, acceptance of) unions may not be a constant through time. A major change in this regard could be held to constitute the major threat to union density in the UK, given that existing recognition arrangements are generally viewed to be largely the result of management (and government) policies and practices.(24)

Increased Management Opposition to Unions?

The work of organisation theorists suggests that organisations change from one ideology or belief system to another because of (i) externally driven crises, (ii) leadership changes and (iii) the properties of ideologies themselves.(25)   The latter factor might suggest that employers could be motivated to move away from an acceptance or tolerance of unions if this ideology became increasingly costly to them.   In the United States a number of studies have suggested that the relative wage effect of unions has increased quite considerably through time, from a 10-15% effect in the 1950s and '60s to some 25-30% by the end of the 1970s.(26)   Furthermore, Freeman and Medoff have estimated that around 40% of the rise in management opposition to union recognition (as proxied by the level of unfair labor practices) in recent decades in the US is due to this increased union relative wage premium.(27)   There are inevitable difficulties in conducting union relative wage studies, with the size of the resulting estimates being extremely sensitive to the level of aggregation of the study and the inclusion (or exclusion) of particular observations. However, the most comprehensive set of evidence on this matter for Great Britain is set out in Table 1.5.

The contents of Table 1.5 indicate that the size of the union mark-up in Britain has increased substantially through time, with it currently being some 2 to 3 times as high as it was in the 1960s; high unemployment and the move to single employer bargaining structures are arguably the major factors behind this substantial increase.

These figures would certainly suggest that management has an increased cost incentive to try and move away from a union acceptance ideology at the organisational level.   At the level of the

Table 1.4: Changes in Import Penetration/Export Sales Ratios and in the Number of Employees, Production and Productivity, UK Manufacturing, 1971-1982

Industry	Change in Import/Export Ratio	1982 employment as % of 1971	Productivity change, 1971-1982	Index of production, 1982 as % of 1971
Vehicles	+0.55	68.3	+14.0	78.1
Other manu-facturing	+0.53	72.0	+32.1	97.0
Metal goods	+0.48	75.0	- 7.4	69.1
Clothing	+0.44	60.0	+39.5	88.6
Textiles	+0.40	50.5	+20.8	61.9
Bricks	+0.40	68.7	+17.6	82.5
Electrical engineering	+0.34	79.9	+55.4	134.2
Leather	+0.33	61.7	-11.0	54.7
Mechanical engineering	+0.24	69.3	+17.0	83.1
Instrument engineering	+0.18	78.3	+33.2	110.1
Chemicals	+0.10	89.2	+31.2	121.0
Metal manu-facture	+0.09	53.0	+24.1	65.3
Coal and petroleum	-0.25	59.1	+28.8	75.6
Paper, printing	-0.25	83.6	+13.9	95.8
Shipbuilding	-0.85	76.2	- 1.3	75.2
Food	-1.75	80.8	+33.0	110.6

Timber   -4.67   76.7   + 8.8   83.9

Source: Michael Chisholm, 'De-Industrialisation and British Regional Policy',
Regional Studies, Vol. 19, No. 4, August 1985, p.309.

Table 1.5:   How Being a Union Member Protects Wages

Period	Union Mark-Up
1960s	4.7
1970s	7.5
1980-1983	11.1

Source: David Metcalf and Stephen Nickell, 'Will
Pay Cuts Bring More Jobs?', New Society, 28th
February, 1985.

---

individual organisation it is widely accepted that
fundamental changes in organisation culture are
most likely to be associated with leadership
changes in the management hierarchy.   However, in
considering changes in ideology across organisations
the leadership influence has been much less systematically studied.   The fact of the matter is that
we know remarkably little about the nature of
inter-organisation influence patterns in terms of
industrial relations.   One possibility, however,
is that the household name, non-union firms in the
UK (e.g. IBM and Marks and Spencer) have become,
as a result of their reputations as 'companies of
excellence', increasingly the pattern setters in
terms of employment practices and arrangements;
they have tended, in other words, to replace the
unionised 'pace setters' of the 1970s (e.g. ICI)
in terms of providing a best practice model to
emulate.   A specific example of this is contained
in a recent article in The Economist (24th August
1985) which reported that IBM and other US owned
non-union firms in Britain have joined with others,
including Kodak and ICL, to form the 'UK Attitude
Survey Group' (an offshoot of the US 'Mayflower'
group set up in the 1970s) to compare the results
of individual employee attitude surveys.   In
addition, the Government, through its treatment of
public sector employees, can perform a potentially
important 'leadership by example' role.   In the UK
the present Government has certainly broken from
the tradition of encouraging union membership
among its own employees in order to set an example
to the private sector.   Indeed, as we shall
see, the example that they would like to set is
arguably the opposite of this traditional one,
although the extent of their influence will
obviously depend on the ability of organisations
to move in this direction.

This question of the ability to move towards non-union structures is an all-important one. In other words, one needs to consider not only the possible incentives for a change in this direction (e.g. the rise in the union relative wage effect, the increased competitive pressures for flexible working arrangements, the potential new 'opinion leaders', etc.) but also the conditions that would be necessary to enable such a change of direction. This point was made quite explicitly in a recent comment on the move towards non-union structures in the United States:(28)

> Under the same set of competitive and demo-
> graphic pressures, other national systems
> have responded differently ... There are two
> major explanations for the differences:
> the different legal framework for industrial
> relations, and the role of public policy.
> Peculiarities of the American system of
> collective bargaining have allowed management
> to seek a non-union alternative or not to
> recognize unions. In most other Western
> nations, going non-union to cut costs is not
> an option.

The view of these authors was that sub-contracting (rather than going non-union) would be the more feasible means of reducing labour costs in Europe; a recent paper by John Atkinson certainly reports that companies in the UK have reduced their 'core' employees and now employ workers on different bases, those without core rights having restricted contracts and being numerically flexible, with greater use of sub-contracting and fixed term employment also being evident.(29) However, as already noted, the UK's movement away from the centralised bargaining arrangements of the 'European model' of industrial relations would appear to have enhanced the ability of organisations to operate on a non-union basis. A further major potential determinant of the capacity to move in the non-union direction will be the nature of the industrial relations legislation (and associated administrative arrange-ments) in existence at any point in time. One needs to stress 'at any point in time' here because an incoming Government may have a mandate to repeal at least some of the industrial relations legis-lation of its predecessor; in this sense one also needs to consider the differing existence and strength of longer term factors (e.g. size of the economy, the existence of regional opposition in individual countries to unions, the relative mixture of multi-establishment and single establishment companies in the industrial structure, etc.) that shape the capacity of organisations to operate as non-union establishments in different systems of industrial relations.

Given the present mixture of incentives and enabling conditions (which will be explored more fully in subsequent chapters), what is the likelihood of a reasonably widespread diffusion of changes in management attitudes and behaviour that are likely to work against the maintenance of overall union density in the UK?   In terms of a priori views there are already disagreements apparent in the literature.   On the one hand it has been suggested that 'the sophisticated paternalist companies, especially those that are foreign owned, are increasingly used as a model for employee relations policies, as witnessed by the growth in quality circles'.(30)   In contrast it has been stated that this particular management style is unlikely to spread much beyond the new, high technology industries, if only because this approach '... requires considerable management resources and a growing, or at least secure, demand for the product to be successful'.(31)   As is so often the case, a priori arguments can be advanced in favour of both sets of views.

One could argue that the paternalist example could, at least in principle, spread quite widely across to establishments of the 'standard modern' pattern.(32)   This is because this category of establishment, which is held to constitute the largest single group in the UK, is very susceptible to such influence because of its essential absence of longer term, industrial relations principles, i.e. its short run opportunism means, almost by definition, that it is very amenable to the 'influence of the moment'.   One of the major reasons for the industrial relations orientation of such firms being subject to considerable short run change and variation is the mixture of 'unitary' and 'pluralist' views held within the management hierarchy both within and between the individual establishments of such companies.   And at the present time (and for the foreseeable future) it is difficult not to conclude that the management functions with a generally unitarist (pluralist) viewpoint have the most (least) influence within senior management decision making circles.

The intra-management tendencies in this regard
are well illustrated by the changing fortunes of
the personnel management function. The 1970s was
typically held to be one of the 'golden ages' of
the personnel function in the UK, with improvements
in their status and authority resulting from the
passage of a substantial volume of employment
legislation, the movement to single employer
bargaining structures and the increased union
density of these years. In fact, the extent of
their gains in status and authority in these
years can easily be exaggerated. We do acknowledge
the increased presence of personnel directors, and
the self-reported status increases of personnel
respondents in various surveys, but nevertheless
note that there is, for example, little evidence
of the personnel function influencing the strategic
decisions of senior management within organisations.(33) The PSI/DE/SSRC workplace industrial
relations survey of 1980 also indicates that the
personnel function was far from being a specialist
function, involving trained individuals, at the
establishment level even by the end of the '70s;(34)
only about 1 in 4 of the senior persons responsible
for industrial relations/personnel matters at the
establishment level were full-time, qualified
individuals. And even the gains that were made
during the 1970s are likely to have been substantially checked, if not reduced since then; this
view has certainly been suggested in a number of
the recent annual reports of ACAS. Admittedly,
the evidence in support of this contention is
little more than anecdotal at this stage. The
likelihood of change in this direction has,
however, considerable intuitive appeal, if only
because an environment of slack labour market
conditions and falling union membership has never
assisted the cause of the personnel management
function. It might also be argued that personnel
has suffered in the '80s from a backlash against
the general belief that line management had lost
too much authority relative to staff management, a
situation that had to be rectified. Even the
alleged growth of quality circles in recent years
does not appear to be particularly associated with
the personnel function; some recent research
indicates that the all important facilitator role
in such circles is, for example, more likely to
come from quality control or production than from
the personnel or training function.(35)

The recent survey findings of Edwards do not necessarily contradict this general view in that much of his evidence concerns 'labour relations matters' or considerations, rather than the personnel/industrial relations function per se;(36) the general move towards flexible working arrangements, for example, is certainly likely to ensure that labour relations considerations remain important, but perhaps disproportionately so for line management.

Those supporters of the alternative view that a widespread management reaction against unionised structures is unlikely to occur in the UK could cite several arguments to this effect. The first argument would be the traditional one that management in the UK is much less anti-trade union than its counterpart in the United States; this is considered more in Chapter 2. A second argument would be that union density in the UK only reached its highest level some six years ago and therefore to talk of, or examine, the issue of union decline due to management opposition is rather premature, not to say foolish; particularly so given the growth of closed shop and check-off arrangements in the 1970s (see Chapter 7) which were indicative, at least in certain cases, of relatively favourable management attitudes towards the institution of unionism. Moreover, reference could be made to the recent research of Batstone which showed that (i) in only a few cases had management attempted to remove the institutional basis of union organisation in the plant; and (ii) in only about 20 per cent of the plants surveyed had management attempted to reduce the role of the union, largely through a reduction in the scope of bargaining and in the degree of shop steward influence over work organisation and earnings;(37) the Edwards survey findings are highly consistent with such results. In fact when one recalls that Batstone was surveying relatively large sized plants in the manufacturing sector only some 4 years after the peak level of union density in the UK had been reached, his latter findings (i.e. 1 in 5 plants seeking to reduce the union role) may not be quite the source of comfort (to the union movement) that some commentators have assumed to be the case. In practice what the Batstone research does, albeit unconsciously, is to indicate that one must be very precise about just where and what one is looking for in considering the whole possibility of an anti-union management move in the UK.

The Possible Signs and Manifestations of Change

There has been much debate in the organisational literature over the question of whether structure follows strategy, or vice versa. This sort of debate over the nature of change in an individual organisation would certainly be replicated in a setting where consideration was being given to the question of change in a national system of industrial relations. In view of this fact one could envisage that if any national system of industrial relations was moving, for want of a better term, in an anti-union direction this would manifest itself at the organisational level in a variety of possible ways, although the exact timing, order, or sequence of these manifestations of change could be a matter of some disagreement. The view adopted here is that a large scale dismantling of existing union structures is arguably the change indicator that is least likely to manifest itself in the early stages of such a move; in other words, to look for (and empirically refute) the large scale lapsing of closed shop and union recognition arrangements in Britain at present is to do little more than set up a 'straw man'. Prior to changes of this type (e.g. the decertification of closed shops or individual bargaining units etc.), one is more likely to see an initial period(s) of (i) priority and behavioural change (on the part of management) with regard to existing unionised structures; (ii) increased management resistance to union attempts to achieve recognition for previously uncovered bargaining units; and (iii) the increased incidence of non-union firms in the system at large. The research presented in this book is very much survey based, covering indicators (ii) and (iii) above. However, given the likely importance of (i) as an early change indicator some attention is given to it here, if only in the hope that this may encourage future research ventures. This research would need to focus on the operation of both 'distributive' and 'integrative' bargaining bodies. As an illustration let us take an example from the latter category. In this case previous research of joint health and safety committees suggested that the priority attached to, and behavioural patterns associated with, such committees could be usefully revealed through the following measures:

23

(i)   the frequency of meetings;
(ii)   the average length of meetings;
(iii)   the proportion of members attending an
         average committee meeting;
(iv)   the circulation (or not) of minutes of the
         committee beyond the membership by means
         other than notice-board postings;
(v)   the existence (or not) of arrangements for
         ensuring that externally (to the plant)
         produced information and documents of
         relevance were passed as a matter of course
         to committee members;
(vi)   the respective numbers of items raised by
         management and union representatives in a
         typical meeting;
(vii)   the degree to which major recommendations
         decided in committee were in fact imple-
         mented.

If pronounced and widespread changes away
from these sorts of characteristics of existing
unionised structures are observed (through longi-
tudinal orientated case studies or survey 'snap-
shots' at dispersed points in time) with little in
the way of compensating changes elsewhere, then one
could reasonably claim to have identified a set of
priority and behavioural changes on the part of
management that are certainly not favourable to
the operation, and possibly the maintenance, of
such arrangements.   The question would then
become whether such management initiated changes
derived solely from their dissatisfaction with the
specific workings of these bodies or whether they
were a particular manifestation of a more general,
adverse reaction against unionised structures.
The influence of the latter would certainly be
suggested by the existence of increased management
resistance to attempts to organise new bargaining
units.

As well as considering management opposition
to attempts at further recognition in partially
unionised establishments we will pay considerable
attention to the question of whether the population
of non-union firms in the UK is on the increase.
This attention seems well overdue as the whole
subject of non-union firms has received remarkably
little attention from industrial relations scholars
in the UK.

The Subject of Non-Union Firms

The standard textbook treatment of industrial
relations in the UK does little more than mention
non-union firms when briefly considering firms
that are not affiliated to employers associations.
Admittedly, Fox's list of industrial relations
patterns does contain a 'traditional pattern',
which represents the non-union sector. The very
term is an unfortunate one given its obvious
connotations, while the category itself covers
such a heterogeneous population that it has little
in the way of explanatory or predictive power.
There have been conceptual refinements of this
particular category which essentially involve a
distinction being drawn between traditionalists and
sophisticated paternalists.(38) The one attempt
at empirical verification of differences in management style went further and postulated a three-way
division (among establishments not recognising
unions) based on the variables listed in Table 1.6.

Table 1.6: Variables and Non-Union Management Style

Variables/Style	(1) Sophisti-cated paternalist	(2) Paternalist	(3) Anti-Union
Consultative committee	Yes	Yes	No
Information on manning	Yes	Yes	No
Clocking-on	No	No	Yes
Procedure for disputes	Yes	No	No
Job evaluation	Yes	No	No
Specialist personnel manager	Yes	No	No

Source: David Deaton, 'Management Style and Large
Scale Survey Evidence', Industrial Relations
Journal, Vol.16, No. 2, Summer 1985, p.70.

The results indicated only a slight tendency
for managerial characteristics to cluster round
the three ideal types, a fact which obviously
raises important questions about the value of
existing conceptual treatments of management style
in the UK industrial relations literature. The
relevant US literature does not appear to offer a

great deal more in this regard.   There a
distinction is typically drawn between a low
standards employer who utilises a union suppression
strategy and a better standards employer who
follows a union substitution approach.(39)   This
dichotomy, however, is very much based on illustrative examples and case studies with little
empirical work, along the lines of Deaton, having
been undertaken on sizeable and representative
data sets.   As a result, the extent to which these
two strategies or sets of tactics for union
avoidance may overlap in practice (as opposed to
constituting discrete, alternative approaches),
is essentially unknown.   Furthermore, the whole
question of the incentives and enabling conditions
that lead firms to seek and maintain non-union
status is remarkably under-researched.   In the
United States considerable research attention has
been given to the influences on the individual
employee decision to unionise, but little has been
given to the motives of firms (owners and senior
managers) seeking non-union status.   In both the
US and the UK literature there is a marked tendency
to explain the contemporary non-union status of
individual firms by reference to little more than
the values of key management individuals in
previous periods of time;   in this sense there is
a strong link with a good deal of the literature
on organisation culture.   These matters will be
explored at some length in Chapter 5.

The Plan of the Book
As indicated by the title, this book is overwhelmingly about the extent of trade union
organisation in the UK.   However, Chapter 2
does discuss at considerable length the decline in
union density (and the alleged reasons for this)
in the private sector in the United States over the
last two decades.   The rationale for this exercise
will be spelt out at some length in the introductory section of that chapter, although here we
simply note the increased union complaints in the
UK of strong anti-union management attitudes and
tactics being transferred from the United States.
        Following Chapter 2 we turn to examine the
experience with statutory union recognition
provisions in Great Britain in the years 1976-1980,
and in Northern Ireland, both then and in subsequent
years.   The emphasis there is on identifying both
the extent and nature of management opposition to
union recognition, with this leading on to some

consideration of both the possible future role and shape of such provisions in the UK. In Chapter 4 we continue the review of management opposition to union recognition through an examination of current experience under voluntary conciliation arrangements. This chapter also examines various voluntary union initiatives in this regard, most notably the EETPU approach of trying to negotiate single recognition agreements in new plants and the BIFU experience in building societies where staff associations have recently emerged as a potentially important alternative to 'external' union representation. Chapter 5 initially outlines the management approach and employment practices of the 'household name' non-union companies in the UK (e.g. IBM), and then goes on to present various pieces of evidence concerning the employment practices and attitudes of US owned establishments and small, single independent businesses in the UK. These two categories of establishments are held to be the major potential additions to the stock of non-union plants and firms in the UK. In Chapter 6 we consider the future for trade union organisation in the public sector, at least as it is attempting to be shaped by the present Government. The possible 'influence by example' role of the Government in this regard will also be considered. Chapter 7 then departs from the orientation of previous chapters, where the concern was with attempts to increase union density through means of increasing the number of recognised bargaining units, by considering attempts to raise union density in existing organised units. This approach involves trying to reduce the difference between the number of employees covered by collective bargaining arrangements and the number that are union members. An examination of attempts to reduce this gap, which is a considerable sized one in the UK, leads us to consider the future of closed shop arrangements. The final chapter draws together the various findings of the book, identifies certain areas or issues as requiring future research and offers a number of suggestions that may be of some interest to anyone concerned about the future extent of union organisation in the UK.

This book does not fit neatly into the traditional pattern of industrial relations books in the UK. Such books frequently tend to be at the opposite ends of a spectrum; there are the

standard textbooks providing a synthesis of others'
research, or there are intensive detailed studies
of a particular subject based on a single research
project.   This book aspires to something of a
middle ground position between these two extremes
in that it very largely constitutes the drawing
together and development of the results and findings
of a number of separate, but related research
projects conducted by the author over a period of
some 7-8 years.   In it a variety of different
data sources and methods of analysis are utilised,
ranging from the quantitative analysis of postal
questionnaire returns to detailed discussions with
individual trade union officers and personnel
managers held over a number of years.   The sort
of book that is being aimed at is, unfortunately,
relatively rare in the field of industrial
relations in the UK, but is probably best represented by George Bain's work on white collar unions.
It is also worth noting that this book draws quite
considerably on the work of scholars outside the
field of industrial relations.   There is more
reference to the organisation theory literature and
to the work of urban and regional scholars on
matters such as new firm formation than has
typically been the case with books on industrial
relations in the UK.   It is difficult to believe
that this will not become an increasingly desirable
tendency in the area of industrial relations
research.

NOTES

1.   Michael Rose, Re-Working the Work Ethic,
Batsford, London, 1985, p.134.
2.   Charles Handy, The Future of Work, Basil
Blackwell, Oxford, 1984, p.128.
3.   Kenneth Walsh, "Trade Union Membership
Statistics in the UK and Ireland", Industrial
Relations Journal, Vol. 16, No. 1, Spring 1985,
pp.25-32.
4.   Allan Barker, Paul Lewis and Michael
McCann, "Trades Unions and the Organisation of
the Unemployed", British Journal of Industrial
Relations, Vol. XXII, No. 3, November 1984,
pp.391-404.
5.   R. Hyman, "Wooing the Working Class",
New Socialist, September/October 1983, pp.41-43.

6.   See, for example, David Bright, Derek
Sawbridge and Bill Rees, "Industrial Relations of
Recession", Industrial Relations Journal, Vol.14,
No.3, Autumn 1983, p.27.

7.   This section is very much based on
R. Price and G.S. Bain, "Union Growth in Britain:
Retrospect and Prospect", British Journal of
Industrial Relations, Vol. XXI, No. 1, March 1983,
pp.46-68.

8.   See Everett M. Kassalow, "The Future of
American Unionism: A Comparative Perspective",
The Annals of the American Academy of Political
and Social Science, No. 473, May 1984, p.56.

9.   Cited in David Metcalf, "On the Measurement of Employment and Unemployment", National
Institute Economic Review, No. 109, August 1984,
p.66.

10.   See John Purcell, "The Management of
Industrial Relations in the Modern Corporation:
Agenda for Research", British Journal of Industrial
Relations, Vol XXII, No. 1, March 1984.

11.   Doreen Massey and Nicholas Miles,
"Mapping Out the Unions", Marxism Today, May 1984,
pp.19-22.

12.   Labour Research, New Technology Special,
Vol. 72, No. 11, November 1983, pp.290-292 and 297.

13.   "Britain's Booming Tribunals", Management
Today, December 1980, p.128.

14.   Linda Dickens et al, "The British
Experience under a Statute Prohibiting Unfair
Dismissal", Industrial and Labor Relations Review,
Vol. 37, No. 4, July 1984, p.505.

15.   Report by the TUC General Council
Industrial Relations Legislation, April 1982, p.18.

16.   G.S. Bain, The Growth of White Collar
Unionism, Oxford University Press, Oxford, 1970,
pp.142-182.

17.   See, for example, Eric Wigham, The Power
to Manage, Macmillan, London, 1973, pp.86-109.

18.   Michael J. Piore and Charles Sabel,
The Second Industrial Divide, Basic Books, New York,
1985.

19.   Charles Handy, Understanding Organizations, Penguin, Harmondsworth, 1985, pp.192-195.

20.   Cited in T.A. Kochan, R.B. McKersie and
H.C. Katz, "U.S. Industrial Relations in Transition"
Proceedings of the Industrial Relations Research
Association, Winter 1984, p.267.

21.   IDS, Group Working and Greenfield Sites,
London, 1984.

22.   P.K. Edwards, "Managing Labour Relations Through the Recession", Employee Relations, Vol. 7. No. 2, 1985, pp.6-7.

23.   Michael Chisholm, "De-Industrialisation and British Regional Policy", Regional Studies, Vol. 19, No. 4, August 1985, p.306.

24.   See K. Prandy, A. Stewart and R.M. Blackburn, White Collar Work, Macmillan, London, 1983.

25.   N. Brunsson, "The Irrationality of Action and Action Rationality: Decisions, Ideologies and Organisational Action", Journal of Management Studies, Vol. 19, No. 1, 1982, pp.29-44.

26.   Robert J. Flanagan, "Wage Concessions and Long Term Wage Flexibility", Brookings Papers on Economic Activity, No. 1, 1984, pp.183-221.

27.   R.B. Freeman and J.L. Medoff, What Do Unions Do?, Basic Books, New York, 1984, p.239.

28.   Janice McCormick and D. Quinn Mills, "Discussion", on Kochan, McKersie and Katz paper, op.cit., p.288.

29.   John Atkinson, "Manpower Strategies for Flexible Organisations", Personnel Management, August 1984.

30.   Purcell, op.cit., p.12.

31.   William Brown and Keith Sisson, "Current Trends and Future Possibilities", in M. Poole et al, Industrial Relations in the Future, Routledge and Kegan Paul, London, 1984, pp.22-23.

32.   Alan Fox, Beyond Contract: Work, Power and Trust Relations, Faber, London, 1974.

33.   See David Hickson and Geoffrey Mallory, "Scope for Choice in Strategic Decision Making and the Trade Union Role", in Andrew Thomson and Malcolm Warner (eds), The Behavioural Sciences and Industrial Relations, Gower, Aldershot, 1981, pp.47-60.

34.   See P.B. Beaumont and D.R. Deaton, "Personnel Management in Britain: Specialisation and Qualifications", Mimeographed paper, 1985.

35.   B.G. Dale, "Quality Circles in the UK: Their Extent and Growth", paper presented to the 1st National Conference of the National Society of Quality Circles, (mimeographed), London, 1983.

36.   Edwards, op.cit., pp.5-6.

37.   See Eric Batstone, Working Order, Basil Blackwell, Oxford, 1984.

38.   J. Purcell and K. Sissons, "Strategies and Practice in the Management of Industrial Relations", in G.S. Bain (ed) Industrial Relations in Britain, Basil Blackwell, Oxford, 1983.
39.   See, for example, Daniel Quinn Mills, Labor-Management Relations, McGraw Hill, New York, 1978, pp.48-66.

Chapter Two

THE MESSAGE FROM AMERICA

To begin a book on the future of union organisation
in the UK with a substantive chapter on the decline
of union organisation in the United States obviously
requires some word of justification. One possible
justification for this starting point would be to
suggest that what is currently occurring in the US
indicates the likely future fate of trade unionism
in the UK. This sort of view would be most likely
to be associated with a commentator who viewed the
shape of future union organisation in any advanced
industrialised economy as being predominantly
shaped by structural or saturationist forces, such
as longer term changes in the industrial and
occupational distribution of the workforce, as
opposed to historical, system specific factors.

The above view would, however, be unlikely to
command a great deal of support among the majority
of industrial relations scholars in either the
United States or the UK. This is because of the
traditional contention or belief that US employers
are _inherently_ more opposed to unions than their
UK counterparts. An argument to this effect is,
for example, contained in the recent book by Phelps
Brown.(1) This is obviously a difficult argument
to formally test on a comprehensive and satisfactory
basis, but the view taken here is that rather too
much can be made of both the _extent_ and _importance_
of this alleged difference in employer attitudes.
In the case of the UK this contention tends to,
firstly, underplay the extent to which union
recognition, particularly for white collar grades
of employees, has only come about as a result of
considerable Government pressure being exerted
through the medium of employers associations in the
wartime periods.(2) And, secondly, it takes
relatively little account of some of the recent

32

work of labour historians, which is unfortunately
not well integrated into mainstream industrial
relations research, that has documented the very
considerable variation in the attitudes and
responses of employers in the UK towards unions;(3)
such variations among employers were often quite
considerable even though they were in the same
industry or area of the country.   It is also worthy
of note that strikes over the issue of 'trade union
principle' were an important component of all major
strikes in Britain well into the 1950s.(4)

One does not necessarily have to fully
subscribe to the view that UK employers are less
inherently opposed to unions than their US counterparts to reject the 'US scenario' as being the
likely future for unions in the UK.   A related,
but more subtle, argument for rejecting this view
is that the UK union movement is a longer established one that has reached levels of workforce
organisation considerably beyond that ever achieved
in the United States.   An argument could therefore
be advanced that this historically higher base
level of union organisation in the UK, which has
created traditions and expectations of minimal
levels of organisation among employers and unions
beyond those in the United States, will underpin
(i.e. through a rachet-type effect) the union
movement in the UK in a way that is unlikely to
occur in the United States.   Certainly Bain's
prediction for the remainder of the decade is that
the level of union organisation in the UK will
revert to the figures of the 1960s (see Table 1.1),
rather than clearly begin to follow the US pattern
of continued decline.(5)   There are other reasons
why one might wish to argue that the level of union
organisation in the UK will not follow the US
pattern or path.   These reasons have essentially
to do with the relatively greater capacity as
opposed to incentive or desire, of employers to
operate non-union in the United States.   The fact
of the matter is that a management wishing to
operate non-union in the United States has a wider
range of options or tactics available to achieve
this end than has his counterpart in the UK.   In
essence, the argument is that in the geographically
smaller economy of the UK there are no regions or
areas of the country with strongly entrenched anti-
union or non-union community or political sentiments
reflected in state level 'right to work' legislation.   This environment, together with certain

pieces of national legislation (such as Part IV of the Employment Protection Act 1975 which requires consultations with unions over redundancies) means that management in the UK, however much it may wish to be non-union, cannot take the full range of actions that are taken for this purpose by management in the United States.

The basic function or purpose of this comparative chapter is therefore to try and identify the full range of actions that management can and has taken to avoid recognising unions in the United States, and then to see how many of these have at least the potential for usage in the UK; in the chapters that follow, we then attempt to identify to what extent this potential has in fact been realised in the UK. In this sense our work fits into the tradition of comparative industrial relations research that is primarily concerned to see to what extent certain findings or occurrences transcend the institutional arrangements of any one system of industrial relations, as opposed to being essentially system specific in nature.

It has recently been argued that the present day US labour movement is facing essentially the same set of problems that it faced in the 1920s.(6) The particular set of problems identified being as follows: (i) a decline in the extent of union organisation; (ii) aged and uninspiring union leadership; (iii) organisational structures made obsolete by changing capital formations; (iv) inability to secure the passage of favourable legislation; (v) failure to stop the technological erosion of unionised work groups; (vi) ineffectiveness against imaginative, aggressive employer attacks upon established bargaining units; and (vii) loss of power in a host of industries in which unions previously had enjoyed considerable bargaining leverage. This sort of view is apparently accepted, at least to a certain extent, by some of the leading trade union officials in the United States. A recent survey of the opinions of nearly 80 such individuals reported, for example, that nearly 70 per cent of them perceived a weakening of union power compared to earlier periods, while only some 27 per cent felt that the future of the labour movement was secure and over half agreed with the statement that there was a crisis in the present day labour movement.(7)

One of the leading alleged causes of this perceived crisis was the hostility of management towards unions. The intensity of the desire of management to avoid unionisation was documented in a conference board survey covering some 670 large, private sector firms.(8)   This data source revealed that avoiding new union organising was the fourth ranked out of 8 possible industrial relations goals for management.   Moreover, 10 per cent of the firms ranked it first, while 30 per cent indicated that it was among their top three criteria for measuring labour relations performance. And those firms giving this particular goal a relatively high ranking were those in which less than 40 per cent of their current workforce was unionised.   Moreover, the latest conference board survey reported that significant declines in union membership in 1977-1983 particularly characterised firms that (i) assigned a relatively high priority to union avoidance, (ii) opened new plants, (iii) introduced workplace innovations in non-union facilities, and (iv) lacked the presence of a dominant union representing employees anywhere in the firm.(9)
This latest survey provides some indication of the particular ways in which this opposition to unions has been manifested.   In fact it appears that one can usefully consider three sequential stages of opposition to unions;   (i) that prior to a representation election;   (ii) opposition at the election stage;   and (iii) post election stage opposition.   Following the discussion under these three headings we then move on to consider the union response in terms of recruitment and organising activity.   And finally, for reasons that will become obvious in the body of this chapter, we conclude our discussion with a brief look at the public policy position with regard to union recognition in Canada.   However, before turning to our first sub-heading of management opposition, we briefly present some figures on union density in the United States.
In the United States the decline in union organisation is very much a private sector phenomenon.   In 1956 some 34 per cent of private sector (non-agricultural) workers were in unions, whereas in 1980 the figure was just under 24 per cent. The absolute number of union members increased over this period of time, but the increase in the size of the workforce was considerably greater,

hence the decline in union density.   Admittedly,
union density rose from some 12.6 per cent in the
public sector in 1956 to 20.1 per cent in 1976, but
at the same time density fell from 51.3 per cent
to 44.6 per cent in manufacturing and from 29.9
per cent to 20.9 per cent in the non-manufacturing
sector.(10)   This overall decline is expected to
continue with various estimates suggesting that
only around 10 per cent of the private sector
workforce is likely to be in unions by the end of
the century.(11)   Indeed some recent figures
indicate that the absolute number of employed wage
and salary earners in unions actually fell from
20.1 million in 1980 to 17.4 million in 1984.(12)
At the same time the total number of employed wage
and salary earners increased from 87.5 million to
91.3 million, with the result that union density
among employed wage and salary earners fell from
23 per cent in 1980 to 19.1 per cent in 1984.
This particular study produced the following
sectoral breakdown for union density among employed
wage and salary earners in the year ending
September 1984:

All industries	19.1%
Construction	24.3%
Manufacturing	26.5%
Transport, communications and public utilities	39.6%
Wholesale and retail trade	8.2%
Finance, insurance and real estate	2.7%
Services	7.2%
Government	35.9%

In addition to this sectoral variation the
probability of an employee being a union member
varies systematically according to other characteristics, such as sex, age, race, level of schooling,
occupation and region of the country.(13)   These
sorts of differences might suggest that the overall
decline in union density in the United States is
very largely a result of industrial, regional,
occupational and sexual shifts in the composition
of the US workforce over the last two decades.
In fact the available research indicates that
these changes have certainly contributed to this
decline, but that they are far from being the most
important source of this trend.(14)   In seeking
to account for this decline a good deal of research
has been conducted on the two major mechanisms by

which individual employees become union members in
the United States; that is individuals (i) become
employed in a job already covered by a collective
bargaining agreement; or (ii) participate in a
recognition or representation election where the
union is successful and becomes the bargaining
agent for that unit. In Chapter 7 we will have
something to say about mechanism (i), but in this
chapter our discussion will very largely revolve
around the route (ii) above. However, before
turning to the relevant research in this regard we
need to examine our first category of management
opposition to unions, namely that prior to a recognition election.

Prior Election Stage Opposition to Unions

The nature of the opposition to be discussed here is
that which was mentioned in Chapter 1, namely that
of better standards, non-union employers following
a union substitution, as opposed to union suppression, approach. The typical components of this
particular strategy have been identified as the
following:(15)

(i)   wages and fringe benefits equal to, or
        greater than, those paid to comparable
        unionised workers in the industry and/or
        labour market;
(ii)   high rate of investment per worker in
        training and career development;
(iii)   advanced systems of organisational communi-
        cation and information sharing;
(iv)   informal mechanisms for, or encouragement of,
        participation in decision making about the
        way the work is to be performed;
(v)   development of a psychological climate that
        fosters and rewards organisational loyalty
        and commitment;
(vi)   rational wage and salary administration,
        performance appraisal, and promotion systems
        that reward merit, but also recognise the
        relevance of seniority;
(vii)   non-union grievance procedure (usually
        without binding arbitration);
(viii) location of new production facilities in
        rural or other weak union areas wherever
        possible; and
(ix)   in some cases, use of employee selection
        devices to avoid workers most likely to be
        pro-union.

The rationale behind these policies is that of
trying to reduce the economic and psychological
pressures and motives that lead employees to demand
unionism. There is in fact considerable theoretical and empirical support for the likely effectiveness of such policies and practices in
limiting the employee demand for unions. The
early theoretical work of Argyris, for example,
very much views trade unions as an adaptive or
adjustment mechanism demanded by employees in
situations where their on-the-job needs are not
being satisfied in formal organisations.(16) And
the most comprehensive empirical studies of the
individual employee propensity to unionise invariably find considerable support for the role of job
dissatisfaction in 'triggering' a demand for
unions.(17)

These sorts of policies and practices have
long been associated with a number of the 'household
name' non-union firms in the United States; one is
obviously thinking here of IBM and Hewlett-Packard,
both of which are given considerable attention in
Ouchi's discussion of firms operating according to
Theory Z principles and practices.(18) The
associated characteristics of Theory Z organisations
in comparison with other organisations in the
United States, have been listed as follows:

Type A (American)	Type Z (modified American)
Short term employment	Long term employment
Individual decision making	Consensual decision making
Individual responsibility	Individual responsibility
Rapid evaluation and promotion	Slow evaluation and promotion
Explicit, formalised control	Implicit, informal control with explicit formalised measures
Specialised career path	Moderately specialised career path
Segmented concern	Holistic concern, including family

There are detailed case studies of individual
non-union firms outside this household name group
who also follow this union-substitution approach,(19)
but just how widespread it is remains far from
clear. According to Kochan,it is only likely to
be those firms operating in an environment of rapid
growth, high profits and which employ a relatively

highly skilled and trained workforce that are likely
to follow this approach;(20) in other words, the
same type of firms that were associated with
employee representation plans and company unions
in the 1920s.   The failure of this earlier union
substitution approach to survive the 1930s depression might lead the unions to believe, or at least
hope, that history will repeat itself.   However,
the recent study by Quinn Mills (21) showing that
management in non-union establishments are deliber-
ately avoiding seeking wage and other concessions
from their employees is some indication that the
'employee treatment' mistakes of the 1930s will not
easily be repeated.

One recent survey has indicated that relatively
well-developed, internal labour market arrangements
were significantly associated with non-union firms
in the San Francisco Bay area.(22)   However, the
place where this union substitution approach is held
to be most evident in the United States is in the
new plants or 'greenfield sites' of multi-establishment companies.(23)   In the States this is the
phenomenon of what is called 'double-breasting',
whereby a single company is able to operate both
unionised and non-union plants;   at present this
particular phenomenon has little counterpart in the
UK.   It is this particular practice that helps
explain why non-union operations in the United
States are very much associated with new industries,
new companies, and with new plants in some of the
traditional union stronghold industries.   For
example, one recent study of a large manufacturing
company found that some 18 new plants had been
opened in the years 1970-1982, with fully 17 of
these being non-union establishments.(24)   The
increased priority attached to opening new plants
(relative to growth through acquisitions) was
accompanied by a work-restructuring programme which
typically involved (i) organising the workforce
into relatively autonomous work teams;   (ii) wage
systems based on pay-for-knowledge principles;
and (iii) some form of productivity bonus.   Currently, non-union plants outnumber unionised ones in
the company by 2 to 1, with the average age of the
union plants being 47 years compared to only 18
years for the non-union ones.   Accordingly, if
there is in fact a genuine 'new plant design
revolution' in progress in the United States, as is
claimed by Lawler (25), then it is likely that non-
union establishments are disproportionately
involved in this phenomenon.

The Election Stage Opposition

In the previous section we discussed what may be
termed a 'prevention' approach to unionism, whereby
management seek to provide terms and conditions of
employment that prevent the emergence of any
employee demand for unionism.   This contrasts with
the present section where management adopt an approach of trying to 'cure' unionism by choking off
any demand that manifests itself.   The focus of
this discussion is very much on the outcomes of
the union representation elections heard under the
auspices of the National Labor Relations Board
(NLRB) where, according to Freeman,(26) the unions
must organise at least 3 per cent of the workforce
every year in order to offset the natural attrition
rate of the unionised workforce (due to the opening
of non-union plants and the closure of unionised
ones) and maintain overall union density.   The
figures set out below in Table 2.1 certainly
indicate that the unions are not currently achieving
this sort of level of success.

Table 2.1:   The NLRB Representation Election
             Record, 1950-1980 (selected years)

Year	Certifi-cation elections	Union victory rates	Number of voters in union victories	Fraction of non-agricult-ural workforce in union victories
1950	5619	74%	753,598	1.92%
1955	4215	68%	378,962	0.87%
1960	6380	59%	286,048	0.62%
1965	7576	61%	325,698	0.64%
1970	7773	56%	307,104	0.53%
1975	8061	50%	208.313	0.33%
1980	7296	48%	174,983	0.24%

Source: Paul Weiler, 'Promises to Keep: Securing
Workers'Rights to Self Organisation under the NLRA',
Harvard Law Review, Vol. 96, No. 8, June, 1983,
p.1776.

The contents of Table 2.1 indicate two adverse
trends for the unions in representation election
outcomes, namely a decline in the union win rate,
and, secondly, a decline in the number of employees
in elections won by the unions.   The focus of this
section will be on the former, with the latter
trend being considered in a subsequent section.

The Message from America

There have been a considerable number of studies concerned to identify the determinants of the outcomes of these representation elections. The existing studies are a mixture of time series and cross-section work, with the dependent variable taking the form of either the proportion of employee votes in favour of union representation or the basic outcome of the election. A variety of potential determinants have been examined in these studies, but in virtually all of them considerable support has been found for various measures of employer opposition as a major determinant of the resulting outcomes. This employer opposition may be of a legal form or nature, with this being proxied by variables such as the proportion of consent elections, the length of time involved between the petition and election dates, and the presence of management consultants.(27) A number of the existing studies have also documented the increased usage of illegal campaign tactics by management in union representation elections. For example, the work of Weiler has indicated that the number of unfair labor practice charges against employers increased by some 750 per cent in the period 1957-1980 (28); his calculations suggested that a union supporter had about a 1 in 20 chance of being illegally dismissed during the course of a campaign for representation. The long running campaign of the Amalgamated Clothing and Textile Workers Union to achieve organisation in the various plants of J.P. Stevens involved many instances of the usage of such illegal tactics.(29)

In Freeman's analysis unfair labor practices are utilised as a measure of total employer opposition (both legal and illegal forms) to recognition, with his estimates leading to the following conclusion:(30)

> From 1950 to 1980, when unfair labor practices per election increased by sixfold, we ... estimate that the rise in management opposition explains from over a quarter to nearly a half of the decline in union success organising through NLRB elections. Put differently had employer opposition to unionism remained at 1950 levels, our calculations suggest that unions would have organised about twice the proportion of the unorganised in 1980 as they in fact did ...

The increased usage of unfair labor practices by management in union representation elections should occasion little surprise given the results of one piece of cost benefit analysis which has indicated the considerable financial gains to employers of committing such practices.(31)   This particular study went on to summarise the various proposals that have been put forward to try and reduce the economic incentive of employers to commit unfair labor practices.   These proposals were as follows:(32)

(i)   increase the interest charge on backpay awards to levels commensurate with current costs of capital;
(ii)   require the NLRB to use Section 10(i) or 10(j) of the National Labor Relations Act to reinstate employees where there is probable cause to believe that there has been a discriminatory discharge until the merits of the case can be determined;
(iii)   require the NLRB to extensively publicise unfair labor practice violations;
(iv)   award double back-pay to employees unfairly discharged and prevent violators from receiving federal contracts;
(v)   award triple back-pay to employees unfairly discharged and fine repeat violators;
(vi)   require the NLRB to reduce delays in the election procedure in order to reduce the economic gains made possible by such delays.

The NLRB can require representation elections to be re-run or can impose bargaining orders in situations where serious unfair labor practices have been committed.   However, in practice these sanctions appear to have produced relatively limited tangible outcomes for the unions.   First, it appears that the level of union success in re-run elections is even lower than that for representation elections in general; in 1979, for example, unions were certified in less than 30 per cent of re-run elections.(33)   And secondly, some research reported by Weiler suggests that imposed bargaining orders have a less than 10 per cent chance of producing a renewal of the initially negotiated collective contract.(34)   The issue of negotiating a first contract following a representation election is pursued more generally in the next section.

In view of the sort of findings outlined in this section, it is hardly surprising to find arguments to the effect that a change in the law and its enforcement are essential to reverse the falling success rate of unions in NLRB elections; indeed we have already noted some such proposals in relation to the commission of unfair labor practices. The AFL-CIO did in fact seek the following changes through the Labor Law Reform Bill of 1977:(35)

(i)   expedite representation elections to be conducted by the NLRB by setting a time limit for the holding of an election;

(ii)   permit unions to address employee meetings on company property if the employer requires employees to attend meetings there in the context of a union organisational campaign;

(iii)   increase the size of the NLRB from 5 to 7 members, ostensibly to speed the disposition of cases before the board;

(iv)   permit the board to speed its processes of review of decisions by administrative law judges that the board receives on appeal;

(v)   provide that any person (or corporation) found in wilful violation of an order of the NLRB, which results from a charge involving coercion of employees and which is upheld by a court decision, be barred from participation in federal contracts for three years;

(vi)   permit award of double back-pay to employees illegally discharged in the context of an organisational campaign;

(vii)   permit the NLRB to order compensation for employees whose employer is found to have illegally refused to bargain with a union over an initial contract.

The above Bill failed to pass Congress, despite the support of the Carter Administration, largely as a result of an extensive campaign of opposition mounted by certain sections of the business community. This opposition should be seen in the light of the fact that the majority of industrial relations commentators in the United States regarded the proposals of the Labor Law Reform Bill as relatively modest in nature. Quinn Mills, for example, argued that really substantial changes in election outcomes would only be likely if legislation was sought and passed that required employers to remain neutral in union organising campaigns, and which provided for the use of secondary boycotts.(36)   Perhaps the most recent 'radical' proposal is that of Weiler who has argued for a move in the direction of the Canadian system of 'instant' elections whereby bargaining rights are awarded on the basis of the results of the unions' organising drive;(37)   lengthy employer (and union) campaigns prior to holding an election are thereby eliminated.   The apparent gains to the Canadian unions of this system are considered later in this chapter.

Post Election Stage Opposition

Even when the unions are successful in winning representation elections there is no guarantee that this will automatically result in the establishment of a longer term collective relationship. According to Philip Ross, an initial collective agreement is unlikely to be negotiated in the face of persistent employer opposition to recognition, following a union representation election victory. (38)   This expectation was confirmed by some figures for the period 1970-1975 which revealed that some 22 per cent of the bargaining units where the unions won representation elections were never brought under contract, while a further 13 per cent were initially brought under contract but this position was not maintained.(39)   A second examination of this matter by the AFL-CIO was of representation election wins in the period April 1979 to March 1980;(40)   the results indicated that some 37 per cent of these units did not obtain a collective agreement within two years of the election, while a further 7 per cent did not obtain a renewal of the first contract.   The only academic study of this phenomenon has been by Cooke who examined the first contract status of some 118 bargaining units in which unions had won NLRB elections in the State of Indiana in the years 1979-1980.(41)   The results of this exercise revealed, firstly, that some 23 per cent of these election wins failed to result in first contracts being negotiated.   And secondly, the situations in which first contracts were unlikely to result were disproportionately characterised by procedural delays and employer violations of the National Labor Relations Act;   in contrast, high firm to industry wage ratios, larger election victories, larger bargaining units and participation by national union officials all increased the probability of first contracts being negotiated.

44

In addition to the specific problem of first contracts, there is a more general phenomenon of post election stage opposition stemming from the fact that the NLRA provides for the possibility that a majority of the members of a bargaining unit may wish to change unions, or to opt for no union representation; this being done through an election procedure similar to that for certification. The number of decertification elections has actually increased from 97 in 1948 to 849 in 1977 (the ratio of decertification/representation elections rising from 3 to 9.8 per cent in this period), with the union currently being decertified in approximately 75 per cent of these.(42) The likelihood of decertification appears to be particularly associated with relatively small sized bargaining units, and ones where there is a leadership (possibly employer sponsored or assisted) among the relevant employees in favour of such an outcome.(43) The overall impact of this trend towards decertification should not, however, be exaggerated. The estimates of Dickens and Leonard, for example, suggest that, holding everything else constant, it would take over 15 years for the current rate of decertification to cause a 1 per cent fall in overall union density.(44) Nevertheless, the decertification route to non-union status has been significant in particular company situations. In the case of the Dow chemical company, for example, the number of unionised plants declined from 22 in 1969 to 7 in 1976 as a result of decertification elections;(45) this substantial change was seen to be the result of the firm's policy of individual job enrichment and the up-grading of hourly paid workers to salaried employee status.

The Union Response

It is against this background that the Executive Council of the AFL-CIO voted in 1980 to place more emphasis on organising drives, and a specialist unit was created in the AFL-CIO to assist member unions to plan and conduct organising campaigns. These 'initiatives' notwithstanding, the extent to which the US union movement as a whole has accorded new recruitment a sufficient or adequate priority has been recently called into question. According to John Lawler the nature of (i) the unions' perceptions of their environment and (ii) leadership succession within the movement have prevented them making the necessary strategic adaptations to

operating in an increasingly adverse environment.
(46)   In his view the unions tend to judge their
current performance and effectiveness by reference to increasingly outmoded standards, and
rationalise any adverse occurrences as being beyond
their control.   This sort of selective interpretation of environmental occurrences, when
combined with the relative absence of 'new blood'
in leadership positions (which in its extreme form
can lead to a 'group think' phenomenon a la Janis),
are the key rigidities which lie behind, among
other things, the inadequate commitment to new
organising initiatives.
      The above view receives some empirical support
from a recent study by Voos of the resources that
a sample of unions had committed to organising
activity over the period 1953-1974.(47)   The basic
finding was that the organising activities of
these unions had not kept pace with the growth of
the workforce, as indicated by the fact that
real expenditure on organising activities per non-
union worker had actually fallen by some 30 per
cent over the period in question.   These figures
were used by Freeman in the earlier referenced work
that examined the declining success of unions in
NLRB elections in recent decades.   According to
his estimates around 20 per cent of this decline
was attributable to reduced organising activity
by the unions;(48)   Voos herself, however, has
questioned some of the basis, and interpretation,
of these estimates.(49)
      A number of union leaders and officials have
nevertheless pointed to the existence of some new,
'successful' organising initiatives in recent
times.(50)   An example frequently cited in this
regard is that of hospitals where the majority of
employers only came under the coverage of the NLRA
for the first time in 1974.   In that year unions
won some 60 per cent of representation elections
in hospitals, but by 1978 this figure had fallen
to 42 per cent with estimates suggesting that
'the percentage of unionisation in the industry
nationally will not be significantly different at
the end of the 1980s than it was at the beginning'.
(51)   There has also been reference made to a
number of new, less conventional, organising
initiatives in recent years.   These particular
initiatives can, according to Craft and Extejt, be
grouped under four basic headings:(52)   (i) the
corporate power strategy;   (ii) the collective
bargaining strategy;   (iii) the community acceptance

and integration strategy; and (iv) the co-
ordinated and pooled resource strategy.

The corporate power strategy involves coercing
the relevant firm through the application of
financial pressures and attempts to isolate it
from the business and consumer communities. A
number of these tactics were used by unions in
attempting organisation in the well known anti-
union company, J.P. Stevens. For example, the
ACTWU proposed to contest the board of directors'
elections for New York Life Insurance Company and
Metropolitan Life Insurance Company, each of which
had Stevens directors on its board. As a result of
this union pressure, both firms removed the Stevens
directors and put pressure on Stevens to deal with
the union. A widely advocated tactic has been for
the unions to seek increased influence over the
investment of pension and welfare funds so as to
put pressure on non-union firms by restricting
their flow of investment capital. For example, the
Retail Clerks union and its allies in 1979 threatened to withdraw some $2 billion in deposits and
pension funds from the Seattle First National Bank
unless the bank recognised the union.

The collective bargaining strategy involves a
union using its power in the existing relationship
to negotiate contractual rules that will facilitate
the organisation of new company establishments.
This strategy has been employed in relation to
multi-plant firms seeking to open new plants in
non-union areas of the country, and has often taken
the form of a 'neutrality pledge' requiring the
company to remain strictly neutral and not oppose
a union organising drive at any of the new, non-
union establishments. Such pledges were contained
in, for example, the UAW-General Motors contracts
of 1976 and 1979, the basic steel settlement
agreement of 1977 and the contracts between the
United Rubber Workers and most of the major tyre
manufacturers in 1979. 'Accretion agreements'
have also been negotiated whereby, when a new plant
opens it is viewed as a transfer and extension of
current operations and, in such circumstances,
the union is granted automatic recognition as the
bargaining agent. An example of such an agreement
is the 1979 IUE-GM one in which the company
agreed to recognise the union at new Packard and
Delco plants that manufactured products similar to
those where the union had representation rights.

The third strategy of community acceptance and integration has been employed in parts of the country that lack a tradition of unionisation. In such areas unions have sought to build a basis of support in the community at large in order to try and change unfavourable perceptions of the trade union movement. This may take the form of initiating programmes to deal with a variety of personal needs in the area. For example, the ACTWU has established a programme to bring health and social services to union and non-union textile workers in some 23 communities in the State of North Carolina. The unions may also seek to work with certain 'allied' groups in the community that have already established a presence among the work-force. The Retail Wholesale and Department Stores union in organising the predominantly black work-force in several Alabama food processing plants became heavily involved in that State's Civil Rights Movement which provided an important basis for its organising attempts.

Finally, there is the co-ordinated and pooled resource strategy which typically involves two or more related unions engaging in an organising drive in a particular target area. In such circumstances the unions will share information regarding employer targets and tactics and pool resources to sponsor media campaigns designed to promote unionisation. Well known examples along these lines are the organising drive of the AFL-CIO Building and Construction Trades Department in Los Angeles County in 1978-1980, and the AFL-CIO 'Houston Project' which involved more than 30 unions in a million dollar initiative designed to organise the Houston area in Texas.

The various examples cited above are all well known, which must raise questions as to how typical they are of recent union organising efforts in general in the United States. Certainly Craft and Extejt feel that they constitute only a relatively small proportion of total organising activity, a fact they attribute to the low priority attached to organising in general, the strong attachment to the traditional organising approach, union rivalries and limited resources and expertise. Moreover, these authors suggest that these new initiatives have been far from an unqualified success, which leads them to believe that the union movement will not substantially increase their commitment to such initiatives in the future and that the few initi-atives that do occur will not make a substantial

contribution to increased trade union membership.

A Brief Note on Canada

The substantial economic and labour interdependence
of Canada and the United States might lead one to
believe that the adverse union trends documented
here for the United States would be very largely
mirrored in the Canadian situation.   This is not,
however, the case.

In Canada total union membership increased
by some 150 per cent in the years 1956-1980, with
union density rising from 33.3 per cent to 37.6
per cent.(53)   Furthermore, union density in
manufacturing and construction increased by 2 and
10 per cent respectively in these years, in both
cases exceeding the comparable figures for the
United States.   An examination of the outcome of
representation elections in the federal sector and
for the provinces of British Columbia and Ontario
for the period 1970-1981 indicated that unions were
certified in 70 per cent of cases.   Admittedly,
there was an observed increase in the number of
unfair labor practices, but the vast majority of
certifications did not require the holding of a
representation election.   According to one set of
calculations for British Columbia and Ontario the
annual increase in union density due to newly
certified units was nearly three times as great as
that in the United States.(54)

In seeking to explain these differences
between Canada and the United States a great deal
of stress has been placed on the role of public
policy as a constraint on the means of expression
of any anti-union management sentiments in Canada;
the earlier noted labour law reform proposals of
Paul Weiler should be recalled here.   The essence
of the Canadian public policy approach in this
regard has been summarised as follows:(55)

> While procedures vary among provinces, the
> thrust of Canadian policy is to encourage
> employee choice without inviting or encour-
> aging protracted employer campaigns.   Most
> jurisdictions rely on signed membership cards
> rather than on elections to determine union
> representation.   Even in jurisdictions where
> elections are preferred to membership cards,
> steps have been taken to expedite elections.
> For example, in Nova Scotia, 'Instant votes'
> are held within five days of an application

for certification in order to combat protracted campaigns. Unions win approximately 75 per cent of these elections.

The emphasis of the Canadian public policy approach is, above all else, on minimising the time involved in reaching a decision on union certification. And from the union point of view the 'virtues' of such an approach follow from the fact that the available evidence, from the United States and (as we shall see) the UK, indicates that the longer the time involved in reaching a decision on this matter, the less likely a union is to achieve recognition.

These Canadian procedures might be argued to produce an 'artificially high' union certification rate which is more than offset by a relatively low level of first (and subsequent) contracts being negotiated; the nature of the procedures could, in other words, lead Canadian employers to concentrate the bulk of their opposition to recognition in the post-certification stage. This is certainly a possibility that warrants detailed examination, but the available data, albeit somewhat limited in nature, does not obviously support such a belief. (56)

Comparative studies that seek to identify a 'universalist' best practice policy that can be readily transferred across to other national industrial relations systems clearly need to be viewed with some degree of caution. Nevertheless it is worth noting that these Canadian union certification procedures have begun to attract increasing interest among US industrial relations scholars. And, for reasons that will hopefully become apparent in the next chapter, we would argue that there is some case for both industrial relations researchers and practitioners in the UK giving them somewhat more than a passing glance.

Conclusions

A recent assessment of the US industrial relations system has argued that it is a system in transition with the collective bargaining and job control unionism of the 1930-1960 period increasingly giving way to the 'slow but steady growth of non-union human resource management systems.'(57) This direction of change has been stimulated by pressures for organisational adaptation stemming from an environment of increased competition, shorter product life cycles and rapid technological change. These environmental pressures, which place a premium on flexible working practices and labour cost containment, clearly transcend the United States, but there the management response has taken the form of (i) opposing union attempts to achieve new organisation, (ii) lapsing or decertifying existing union arrangements or structures, and (iii) opening up new plants on a non-union basis; the latter has often involved the introduction of quality of work life measures (e.g. quality circles, autonomous workgroups), while wage and benefit freezes or cutbacks have been sought in existing unionised establishments.

In general this sort of response to these common environmental pressures is not expected in Europe, although at least one individual has suggested that Britain is the most likely country in Europe where this could occur.(58)   The movement away from the centralised collective bargaining pattern of Europe certainly makes this more of a possibility than in the past, although as this and the introductory chapter indicate, a number of other potential facilitating factors also need to be considered.   Accordingly, having developed a checklist in the United States we utilise this as something of a reference point in the chapters that follow.

NOTES

1.   E.H. Phelps Brown, The Origins of Trade Union Power, Clarendon Press, Oxford, 1983.

2.   George Sayers Bain, The Growth of White Collar Unionism, Oxford University Press, London, 1970, pp.142-182.

3.   See, for example, P. Joyce, Work, Society and Politics, Wheatsheaf, Brighton, 1980.

4.   J.W. Durean, W.E.J. McCarthy and G.P. Redman, Strikes in Post War Britain, George Allen and Unwin, London, 1983, p.44.

5.   Quoted in David Bright, Derek Sawbridge and Bill Rees, "Industrial Relations of Recession", Industrial Relations Journal, Vol.14, No.3, Autumn 1983, p.32.

6.   Charles Craypo, "The Decline of Union Bargaining Power", in Michael Carter and William Leaky (eds) New Directions in Labor Economics and Industrial Relations, University of Notre Dame Press, Notre Dame, Indiana, 1981, p.108.

7.   Brian Heshizer and Harry Graham, "Are Unions Facing a Crisis?   Labor Officials are Divided", Monthly Labor Review, Vol. 107, No. 8, August 1984, pp.23-25.

8.   Thomas A. Kochan, Collective Bargaining and Industrial Relations, Irwin, Homewood, 1980, pp.187-188.

9.   T.A. Kochan, R.B. McKersie and H.C. Katz, "U.S. Industrial Relations in Transition", Proceedings of Industrial Relations Research Association, Winter 1984, p.267.

10.   Kochan, op.cit., p.128.

11.   Richard B. Freeman and James L. Medoff, What Do Unions Do?, Basic Books, New York, 1984, pp.221-245.

12.   Larry T. Adams, "Changing Employment Patterns of Organised Workers", Monthly Labor Review, Vol. 108, No. 2, February 1985, pp.25-31.

13.   Freeman and Medoff, op.cit., pp.26-34.

14.   Henry S. Faber, "The Extent of Unionisation in the United States: Historical Trends and Prospects for the Future", paper presented to the MIT/Union Leadership Conference, June 1983 (mimeographed).

15.   Kochan, ibid., p.185.

16.   Chris Argyris, Personality and Organisation, Harper and Row, New York, 1958, pp.103-107.

17.   Kochan, ibid., pp.142-149.

18.   William Ouchi, Theory Z, Addison-Wesley, Reading, Mass., 1981.

19.   Fred K. Foulkes, Personnel Policies in Large Non-Union Companies, Prentice Hall, Englewood Cliffs, 1980.

20.   Kochan, ibid., p.185.

21.   D. Quinn Mills, "When Employees Make Concessions", Harvard Business Review, May-June 1983

22.   Jeffrey Pfeffer and Yinon Cohen, "Determinants of Internal Labor Markets in Organisations" Administrative Science Quarterly, Vol.29, 1984, pp.550-572.

23.   Thomas A. Kochan and Harry C. Katz, "Collective Bargaining, Work Organisation and Worker Participation: The Return to Plant Level Bargaining", Proceedings of the Industrial Relations Research Association, Spring 1983, p.528.

24.   Anil Verma, "Union and Non-Union Wages and Management Decision Making in Industrial Relations at the Firm Level", Faculty of Commerce and Business Administration, University of British Columbia, Working Paper No. 1023, 1984.

25.   E.E. Lawler, "The New Plant Revolution",
Organizational Dynamics, Winter 1978, pp.3-12.
26.   R.B. Freeman, "Why are Unions Faring
Poorly in NLRB Representation Elections?" paper
presented to the MIT/Union Leadership Conference
June 1983 (mimeographed) pp.5-6.
27.   Freeman, op.cit., pp.18-19.
28.   Paul Weiler, "Promises to Keep: Securing
Workers Rights to Self Organisation under the NLRA",
Harvard Law Review, Vol.96, No.8, June 1983, p.1781.
29.   Kenneth A. Kovach, "J.P. Stevens and the
Struggle for Union Organisation", Labor Law Journal,
Vol. 29, May 1979, pp.300-308.
30.   Freeman, ibid., pp.24-25.
31.   Charles A. Greer and Stanley A. Martin,
"Calculative Strategy Decisions During Union
Organisation Campaigns", Sloan Management Review,
Winter 1978, pp.61-74.
32.   Greer and Martin, op.cit., p.73.
33.   John A. Fossum, Labor Relations: Development, Structure, Process, Business Publications,
Dallas, Texas, 1982, p.151.
34.   Weiler, op.cit., p.1795.
35.   Quinn Mills, "Flawed Victory in Labor
Law Reform", Harvard Business Review, 1978, p.93.
36.   Quinn Mills, op.cit., p.94.
37.   Weiler, ibid., pp.1806-1822.
38.   Philip Ross, The Government as a Source
of Union Power, Brown University Press, Providence,
Rhode Island, 1965, pp.258-259.
39.   Richard Prosten, "The Longest Season:
Union Organising in the Last Decade", Proceedings
of the Industrial Relations Research Association,
Winter 1978, pp.246-247.
40.   Quoted in Weiler, ibid., p.1810.
41.   William N. Cooke, "The Failure to
Negotiate First Contracts: Determinants and
Policy Implications", Industrial and Labor Relations
Review, Vol. 38, No. 2, January 1985, pp.163-178.
42.   John C. Anderson, Gloria Busman and
Charles A. O'Reilly, "What Factors Influence the
Outcome of Union Decertification Elections?",
Monthly Labor Review, November 1979, pp.32-36.
43.   John C. Anderson, Gloria Busman and
Charles A. O'Reilly, "The Decertification Process:
Evidence from California", Industrial Relations,
Vol. 21, 1982, pp.178-195.
44.   William T. Dickens and Jonathan S.
Leonard, "Accounting for the Decline in Union
Membership", National Bureau of Economic Research,
Working Paper No. 1275, February 1984, p.7.

45. Craypo in Carter and Leaky (eds) op.cit., pp.140-141.

46. John J. Lawler, "Trade Union Strategy in a Time of Adversity", Institute of Labor and Industrial Relations, University of Illinois, Mimeographed Paper, December 1982.

47. Paula B. Voos, "Union Organising: Costs and Benefits", Industrial and Labor Relations Review, Vol.36, No.4, July 1983, pp.576-591.

48. Freeman, ibid., p.12.

49. Paula B. Voos, "Trends in Union Organizing Expenditures, 1953-1977", Industrial and Labor Relations Review, Vol.38, No.1, October 1984, pp.52-63.

50. Alan Kistler, "Union Organising: New Challenges and Prospects", The Annals of the American Academy of Political Science, No. 473, May 1984, p.105.

51. Brian Becker and Richard V. Miller, "Patterns and Determinants of Union Growth in the Hospital Industry", Journal of Labor Research, Vol. 2, No.2, Fall 1981, p.326.

52. James A. Craft and Marian M. Extejt, "New Strategies in Union Organising", Graduate School of Business, University of Pittsburgh, Mimeographed Paper, 1982.

53. Joseph B. Rose and Gary N. Chaison, "The State of the Unions: United States and Canada", Journal of Labor Research, Vol.VI, No.1, Winter 1985, p.98.

54. Rose and Chaison, op.cit., p.102.

55. Rose and Chaison, ibid., pp.103-104.

56. Rose and Chaison, ibid., p.104.

57. Kochan, McKersie and Katz, op.cit., p.264.

58. Jack Barbash, "Discussion" (the above proceedings), p.294.

Chapter Three

THE EXPERIENCE WITH STATUTORY RECOGNITION PROVISIONS

This chapter is very largely concerned with the
operation of statutory recognition provisions in
(i) Great Britain in the years 1976-1980, and (ii)
Northern Ireland in these and subsequent years.
There are a number of reasons for this particular
concentration.   The first is that the very introduction of such provisions constituted a considerable departure from previous UK practice and, as
such, indicated a union concern about future organisation that was prior to and independent of both
the present economic downturn and the policies of
the Thatcher Government.   Secondly, our analysis
of this experience has strong parallels with the
work that has been conducted on the outcomes of
NLRB elections in the United States, which we
reported in the previous chapter, and therefore
should be helpful in revealing the extent and
nature of some of the contemporary management
opposition to union recognition; specifically, we
should be able to identify the extent to which the
various US forms of management opposition that we
have so far discussed have counterparts in the UK
setting.   And finally, we hope to demonstrate,
largely through a consideration of the Northern
Ireland situation, that both the impact of statutory
recognition provisions and their potential for
reform may have been rather underestimated by a
number of industrial relations practitioners and
commentators in the UK.

The Background
The case for introducing statutory recognition
provisions in Great Britain was particularly associated with a number of white collar unions in the
mid to late 1960s.   Prominent among these was
ASTMS who presented such a case in their evidence

to the Donovan Commission.   Moreover, Clive
Jenkins of ASTMS, in a book written with Jim
Mortimer, argued that British trade unions needed
to move beyond their traditional reliance on legal
immunities to a position of seeking a set of
positive legal rights, including that to recognition.   This sort of view was associated with a
number of successful motions at annual meetings of
the TUC (such as in 1966) urging that legislative
expression or backing be given to Britain's
ratification of ILO Convention No.98 which obliges
governments to encourage the fullest possible
development of collective bargaining arrangements.
        In advocating a movement in this direction
unions such as ASTMS were obviously mindful of a
number of significant changes in the British system
of industrial relations in this period of time.
Among the most influential changes in this regard
were, as mentioned in Chapter 1, the movement
towards single employer bargaining arrangements in
the private sector and the changes in the industrial
and occupational distribution of the workforce as
a whole; the latter, as Price and Bain have demon-
strated (1), tending to work against the maintenance
of overall union density.   In addition, the relatively high levels of union density and collective
bargaining coverage in certain parts of the industrial relations system, most notably among manual
workers in manufacturing and among public sector
employees, in the early 1970s must have raised
fears about possible saturation levels being
increasingly close at hand.   These sorts of views
received considerable academic support from prominent researchers such as Bain and Flanders.
        Statutory recognition provisions were in fact
contained in the Industrial Relations Act 1971.
The operation of these provisions was of benefit to
some individual unions, most notably NUBE (now BIFU)
but any more general effect was limited by the
union's policy of non co-operation with the Act;
fully 17 of the 54 Section 45 applications from
unions (13 others came from employers and the
Secretary of State) by April 1974 came from
NUBE.(2)   The existing studies of these provisions,
most notably that by James (3), were important in
revealing the existence of two particular problems
for the unions concerned, namely the influential
effect of time delays on recognition outcomes and
employer non-compliance with third party recommendations in favour of recognition.   These particular
findings do not, however, appear to have much

influenced those responsible for drafting sections
11-16 of the Employment Protection Act 1975, which
are the statutory recognition provisions we now turn
to examine in some detail; the sanction for
employer non-compliance with a recommendation for
recognition, for example, was exactly the same in
both the 1971 and 1975 Acts.

The Section 11-16 Provisions

These statutory provisions, which operated in Great
Britain from February 1976 to August 1980, allowed
an independent trade union to refer a recognition
issue to the Advisory Conciliation and Arbitration
Service (ACAS). ACAS then had a duty to examine
the issue, to seek to resolve it by conciliation
if appropriate and, failing that, to make further
inquiries and prepare a written report. In addition to obtaining the obvious benefits of recognition, an independent union also received certain
related rights, such as those pertaining to time
off for trade union duties and activities, to dis-
closure of information for bargaining purposes, to
consultation on the procedures for handling redundancies and to appoint safety representatives.
The available procedures appeared to give ACAS
wide discretion and flexibility in pursuing its
recognition inquiries, and reaching its conclusions,
although it was required to:

(i)   Give regard at all times to the desirability
        of encouraging the settlement of the issue
        by agreement and where appropriate to seek
        to assist a settlement by conciliation;
(ii)   Consult all parties who it considered would
        be affected by the outcome of the reference;
(iii)   Prepare, if the issue was not settled and
        the reference not withdrawn, a written
        report setting out its findings, any advice
        in connection with these findings, and any
        recommendations for recognition, with
        reasons, or the reasons for making no
        recommendations;
(iv)   Specify in any recommendation the employer,
        trade union and description of workers, to
        whom it related, whether it was for recog-
        nition generally or in respect of specified
        matters,(e.g. wages, hours, bargaining only)
        and the level at which recognition was
        recommended (e.g. only matters falling
        within the discretion of plant level
        management).

57

The Act provided that a trade union which had received a recommendation for recognition could complain to ACAS of any non-compliance by the employer. In certain circumstances, such a complaint of non-compliance could lead to a unilateral arbitration award by the Central Arbitration Committee (CAC) requiring the employer to incorporate terms and conditions into his employees' individual contracts of employment.

In Table 3.1 we set out the total number of Section 11 recognition references that went to ACAS, in the years 1976-1980, the particular stage at which they were settled, and their outcome.

The contents of Table 3.1 indicate that the overwhelming majority of recognition references were settled at the initial (Section 11) conciliation stage of the procedure. Indeed, there were only 247 references that went through to the full, published Section 12 report stage out of the total of 1,610 references. At the Section 11 stage, just under half (47 per cent) of the 1,115 settlements resulted in the union being fully or partially successful in securing recognition. The union 'success rate' at the full statutory Section 12 stage was greater, with approximately 65 per cent of the reports recommending full or partial recognition. However, as we shall see, the ultimate union success rate was probably much greater at the Section 11 than the Section 12 stage, in that a high proportion of the Section 12 recommendations for recognition were not, in fact, implemented by the employer concerned.

The industries which stood out in terms of the proportion of claims accounted for by them were food, drink and tobacco manufacture, mechanical engineering, the distributive trades, professional and scientific services and miscellaneous services. For the period as a whole, these five industry orders accounted for just under 43 per cent of the total number of Section 11 references. The stability of industry rankings in the use of these procedures for individual years was assessed by computing Spearman (rank) correlation coefficients. All coefficients (which ranged from 0.52 to 0.89) were statistically significant, indicating that the high (low) industry users in one year were the same high (low) users in the other years. The number of claims in the period 1976-1980 by individual industry were regressed on the proportion of manual and non-manual employees covered by collective bargaining arrangements, together with the propor-

Table 3.1   Total Number of References under
             Section 11 with their State of
             Settlement and Outcome
             (1st February 1976 - 15th August 1980)

Stage	Outcome	Number
Section 11	Full recognition accorded to union as a result of its application	306
	Partial recognition or representational rights accorded and accepted by union as satisfactory	143
	Union claim to recognition withdrawn because of low membership and support	336
	Union claim withdrawn for other reasons	195
	Section 11 application withdrawn for further negotiations between union and employer where union has been unsuccessful in securing recognition	13
	Application for reference withdrawn for technical reasons	53
	References where inquiries (conciliation, survey etc) were taking place prior to draft report	220
	References where draft reports were under consideration	28
References reported on under Section 12		247
Total references		1,610

Source: ACAS Annual Report 1980, HMSO, London,
           1981, Tables 17 and 19.

tion of total employment accounted for by each
industry. The results obtained indicated that the
recognition claims were disproportionately concentrated in industries with relatively low levels of
white collar collective bargaining, whereas the
manual recognition claims were more randomly distributed across industries. These results were
consistent with the pattern of individual trade
union usage of the provisions. More than a third
(34.5 per cent) of all recognition references were
accounted for by only two unions, 48 per cent by
four unions and 64 per cent by seven unions. The
heavy user unions were, in order of usage, the
TGWU, ASTMS, AUEW-TASS, APEX, AUEW, GMWU and ACTSS.
The ACAS Annual Report for 1980 estimated that
recognition had been accorded to approximately
65,000 workers as a direct outcome of all Section
11 references.(4) By making some adjustments to
this figure it is possible to estimate the contribution of these provisions to total union membership
growth in the years 1976-1980. If one deflates
this figure of 65,000 by some 19 per cent, as an
estimate of the extent to which collective agreement coverage exceeds union density (19 per cent
is the mid-point of the differences between these
two measures in 1973 and 1978), then these provisions appear to have accounted for some 9.4 per
cent of the total trade union membership increase
of 561,000 in the years 1976-1980.
This relatively small sized contribution
should not, as such, be interpreted as indicating
the failure of the statutory recognition provisions.
The point here is that statutory recognition provisions when introduced relatively late on in the
history of an industrial relations system with a
relatively high level of overall union density are
not intended, or likely, to be a major vehicle for
union recognition in a numerical sense. Their
potential value to a union movement in such circumstances is as a back-up or last resort measure
allowing them to penetrate areas of employment
that have proved resistant to organisation attempts
using traditional means. Accordingly, their
practical achievements need to be assessed in
relation to three measures:

(i)   Is there a significant concentration of
        recognition claims in the little organised
        sectors of the labour market? (The ind-
        ustry level regression findings reported
        earlier provide some basis for an affirma-

tive answer here.)

(ii)   Is there a significant concentration of
         'successful' claims (i.e. those which inv-
         olve a third party recommendation for
         recognition) in these relatively little
         organised sectors of the labour market?

(iii)   Is there a significant concentration of
         employer compliance with the third party
         recommendation for recognition in these
         relatively little organised sectors of the
         labour market?

In what follows we are specifically concerned to assess the extent to which conditions (ii)
and (iii) were realised.   For this purpose, and to
accord with the approach of our previous chapter,
we examine our material under the headings of ballot
stage and post-ballot stage opposition.

The Ballot Stage Opposition
In considering opposition at the ballot stage one
instinctively tends to think of highly publicised
cases such as that at Grunwick Processing Labora-
tories Limited., where ACAS was unable to obtain
the names and addresses of most of the workers
employed on the premises at the time of the inquiry.
The potential importance of such cases is two-fold.
Firstly, they may have encouraged other employers
not to co-operate with ACAS.   In this regard it is
worth noting that the ACAS Annual Report for 1980
stated that such non co-operation only occurred in
nine of their first 150 cases, but by the time the
provisions were repealed in 1980 it was experiencing such difficulties in over 50 of the 248 out-
standing cases at the time.(5)   This employer
opposition typically centred on the form of the
questionnaire, with the employers maintaining that
one or more questions were biased and/or that alternative or additional questions should be asked;   in
particular employers often suggested that workers
should not only be asked whether they would favour
the applicant (or another) union bargaining on
their behalf, but also whether they would prefer
existing arrangements to prevail.   In addition
such cases may have disproportionately contributed to undermining the confidence of ACAS as to
its ability to satisfactorily operate these
provisions.   The position of ACAS was clearly an
important factor in the decision to repeal these
provisions and is therefore a matter returned to
later in this chapter.

However, in this section we need to move beyond the particular circumstances of such highly publicised cases of non co-operation in order to develop a generalised, and indeed generalisable, measure of employer opposition to recognition. This is because our intention is to examine, a la the American work of the previous chapter, the relevant determinants of the outcome of all the recognition claims that went through to the stage of involving a published, Section 12 report; the relatively small number of claims to reach this final stage of proceedings should be recalled here (Table 3.1).

The full set of published Section 12 reports was examined with a view to obtaining all relevant reported data from the results of the ballots of the employees concerned. The result was a set of 249 observations for the recognition claims of individual unions from a total of 228 published reports. In this set of 249 observations there were 38 different unions involved, with the major ones being the Transport and General Workers Union (21.3 per cent), the Association of Scientific Technical and Managerial Staffs (20.5 per cent), the Amalgamated Union of Engineering Workers - Technical, Administrative and Supervisory Section (11.6 per cent) and the Association of Professional, Executive, Clerical and Computer Staff (6.8 per cent). More than half of the cases (56.2 per cent) involved non-manual workers only, 35.3 per cent involved manual workers only, and 8.4 per cent involved both manual and non-manual employees. A quite sizeable range of industries was represented but with the largest individual groups being the distributive trades (12.9 per cent), mechanical engineering (9.6 per cent), food drink and tobacco manufacture and professional and scientific services (both 7.6 per cent), chemicals and allied manufacture (6.8 per cent) and miscellaneous services (6.4 per cent). The basic results of the reports were an ACAS recommendation in favour of full recognition in 59.8 per cent of cases, a recommendation for partial recognition in 4 per cent, and recognition being not recommended in the remaining 36.1 per cent of cases.

In seeking to analyse the outcomes of these recognition claims, the independent variables available to us may be considered as follows on p.64.

The individual variable whose statistical performance is of particular interest to us here is number (vi), that is the length of time involved in hearing and deciding the claim. This is because it is our major measure of the extent of employer opposition to union recognition. The use of this variable for such a purpose can be justified by reference to the results of US studies and that by James of the 1971 Act in Britain. The raw figures certainly lend initial support to the belief that the greater the extent of employer opposition, the longer the time taken to hear and decide a claim and the less likely the union is to win it; the mean length of time from referral to report was 13.1 calendar months in claims where recognition was recommended and 16.5 months where it was not recommended. The full set of correlation results obtained is set out in Table 3.2.

There are some differences between the two sets of results (most notably for the turnout rate variable), but four variables attain varying degrees of statistical significance in both. These four variables were inter-union competition, unit size, non-manual claims, and the length of time involved in hearing and deciding the claim. All four variables have the same signs in both sets of results, indicating that a lower employee vote for the applicant union and no recommendation for recognition were most likely to occur where there was substantial inter-union competition, a non-manual claim, a relatively large sized bargaining unit and a relatively long time taken to hear and decide the claim.

Moreover, further analysis revealed that only 53 per cent of the claims involving non-manual workers received a recommendation for recognition, compared to 73 per cent of claims for manual workers. The low union win rate among these white collar claims was due less to the employees' lack of interest in unionism and collective bargaining in general than to a number of the associated characteristics of these claims. These associated characteristics included a relatively high degree of inter-union competition, relatively large sized bargaining units and a relatively long time taken to hear and decide the claim. In the case of the latter factor we found that the mean length of time taken to hear and decide the non-manual claims was 16.6 months, compared to a mean figure of only 11.3 months for the manual claims.

Sub-Vector	Individual Variable	Relationship to Union Recognition being Recommended
The attractiveness of the individual union seeking recognition	(i) The four unions disproportionately involved in the claims	+
	(ii) The extent of inter-union competition (measured by the difference between the proportion of employees in favour of collective bargaining in general and the proportion in favour of the applicant union)	−
	(iii) The size of the bargaining unit	−
The attractiveness of unionism and collective bargaining in general	(iv) Non-manual bargaining unit	−
	(v) The percentage of eligible employees who voted	+
The extent of employer opposition to recogniton	(vi) The length of time between the date the claim was referred to ACAS and that of the final published report	−

(vii)   The four industries with less than 30 per cent of their male non-manual workforce covered by collective bargaining arrangements

Table 3.2: Correlation Coefficients Between Independent Variables and (i) Percentage of Respondents Voting for the Union and (ii) an ACAS Recommendation for Recognition

Variables	Correlation Coefficients	
	(i)	(ii)
Particular union	+0.11269	+0.14515 **
Inter-Union Competition	-0.38814 ***	-0.29131 ***
Unit size	-0.22155 ***	-0.12433 *
Non-manual	-0.15571 **	-0.17302 **
Turnout rate	-0.18895 ***	+0.01765
Time involved	-0.13704 *	-0.21793 ***
Industry	+0.06740	+0.08614

*   = significant at the .10 level
**   = significant at the .05 level
*** = significant at the .01 level

Source: P.B. Beaumont, 'Statutory Recognition Provisions in Britain, 1976-1980', Relations Industrielles, Vol.38, No.4, 1983

Thus the form of employer opposition documented at the ballot stage largely involved unions seeking recognition for white collar bargaining units in partially unionised establishments. These particular results clearly lend considerable empirical support to the suggestion of Jenkins and Sherman that:(6)

Employer procrastination has been practised widely and ACAS has no powers to deal with it. Some cases have been at ACAS for eighteen months and are still not resolved. This is partly due to under-staffing and partly due to the quality of staffing, although it must, in fairness, be said that many of the old CIR hands who transferred over are both perceptive and diligent. It is, however, basically due to employers delaying ballots, losing computer discs or changing the concept of the bargaining

unit.   Obviously this is in the interests of
the employer ... trade union membership tends
to melt away when recognition is not forth-
coming and this is precisely what is in the so
un-co-operative employers' minds.

The reference to attempts to change the
bargaining unit is particularly important in that
ACAS frequently found themselves attempting to
reconcile employer and union arguments on this
matter.   The employers typically argued for a
wider negotiating group, on the grounds of desiring
to limit fragmentation of bargaining arrangements
or to fit in with existing structures, whereas the
union view was invariably that no individual group
of workers should be denied representation simply
because of a lack of support from other workers in
a more widely defined group; these arguments should
be seen in the light of the Table 3.2 finding that
unions win significantly fewer recognition claims
in relatively large sized bargaining units.   One
approach that ACAS did adopt in such circumstances
on occasions was that of recommending recognition
only in respect of matters falling within the discretion of local management.   This sort of recommendation needs to be seen in the context of
industrial tribunal decisions regarding the degree
of recognition that is necessary before management
has to consult with unions about the procedures for
implementing redundancies.   As a final comment in
this section it is worth noting that an unsuccessful
private members bill sought to limit the hearing
and decision making period to a maximum of six
months.

The Post-Ballot Stage Opposition
As with the American legislation, those drafting
Sections 11-16 of the Employment Protection Act
1975 were conscious that a third party recommendation for recognition would not automatically
guarantee that such would come about.   Section 15
in fact provided that a union could complain to ACAS
after two months from the operative date of a
recommendation, that the employer had failed to
comply with the recommendation.   In such circumstances, ACAS had a duty to attempt conciliation,
but where this failed the union could submit to
the Central Arbitration Committee a claim concerning
terms and conditions of employment.   Under the
terms of Section 16 CAC would hear the complaint
and could make an arbitration award based on the

union's claim.   As mentioned earlier, this unilateral arbitration award of terms and conditions
to take effect through the individual contract of
employment was the same basic sanction that applied
in the case of the Industrial Relations Act 1971.
And James examination of this earlier experience,
which found that only some 50% of the CIR recommendations had been implemented in practice, raised
doubts about its likely effectiveness;   in his view
more influential sanctions might have included the
incorporation of a procedural agreement in an
arbitration award or an award of financial compensation to the union concerned.

The ACAS annual report for 1980 indicated that
the years 1976-1980 witnessed some 50 Section 15
complaints, with 8 of these being successfully
conciliated.   And in the remaining 42 cases, 29
were taken to the CAC with 18 of these resulting in
an award of terms and conditions of employment.(7)
The CAC consistently stated that it lacked the
power to place the employer under an obligation to
recognise the applicant union.   And, as a consequence, they could only seek to minimise the dis-
advantages to the union of the absence of direct
negotiations with the employer.   These disadvan-
tages were, however, viewed in very narrow terms,
namely the loss of substantive rights in relation
to the annual negotiation of pay and hours matters.
(8)   For example, the case of B J & G Limited,
involved an ACAS recommendation in May 1979 that
the company recognise ASTMS in respect of staff
employees.   Following a complaint of non-compliance
with this recommendation the union presented the
following claim to CAC some 4 months later:

(i)   basic pay 25 per cent above present level;
(ii)   reduction in hours to 35 without loss of pay;
(iii)   pay during sickness;
(iv)   one day increase in holiday entitlement;
(v)   a job security agreement;
(vi)   paid release for training of union represen-
        tatives;
(vii)   a technology agreement;
(viii) a check-off agreement;
(ix)   a disciplinary and grievance procedure.

In this case the CAC stated that 'any award
made by us must relate to terms and conditions
which can take effect as part of the contracts of
the employees concerned'.   The result was that
they rejected from consideration items (vi)-(viii)

68

in their entirety, and parts of items (v) and (ix).
Subsequently, the CAC, in their annual report for
1981, acknowledged the disappointing impact of this
particular sanction in recognition disputes.(9)
       The inability of unions as institutions a la
Arthur Ross to gain in procedural terms from this
sanction clearly limited the number of Section 15
complaints relative to the level of actual non-
compliance with ACAS recommendations; in other
words, a simple head-count of such complaints
substantially understated the level of non-compliance.   The evidence in support of this proposition
came from Incomes Data Services who followed up on
all but 5 of the published Section 12 reports.
This exercise involved an extensive series of
telephone inquiries of the unions concerned, with
some occasional cross-checking with employers, some
six months after the date of publication of these
reports.   The basic findings of this examination
were as follows:

Position	Number of Cases
No agreement due to employer non-compliance	88
No agreement due to other circumstances such as plant closure	10
Negotiations still being conducted	30
Partial agreement	5
Full agreement	24
No recommendation for recognition	88
No information (i.e. no follow up)	5

       The above figures indicate that recognition
had only definitely come about in some 18% of the
reports where this was recommended.   Moreover,
there was definite non-compliance in more than half
of the cases where recognition had been recommended
(54%), a figure that could well have risen if some
of the cases in the 'negotiations still being
conducted' category came to nothing.
       According to Ross and Prosten, whose work was
considered in Chapter 2, employer non-compliance
with a recognition recommendation is most likely to
occur in circumstances where (i) there was only a
slight employee majority (in the ballot) in favour
of the union; and (ii) sustained employer opposition existed, as indicated by a relatively long

period of time being taken to hear and decide the original claim. These two suggestions imply that ballot stage and post-ballot stage opposition are likely to be essentially complementary strategies pursued by employers. This is an important matter to investigate as Kochan has also raised the more general question of whether the broad union substitution and union suppression approaches, that we outlined in Chapter 1, are discrete alternatives as opposed to constituting somewhat overlapping strategies pursued by management;(10) arguably, ballot stage opposition is more in the substitution tradition, whereas the post-ballot stage opposition probably better fits under the suppression heading.

Our analysis of this statutory recognition experience in Great Britain suggests that employer opposition at the ballot and post-ballot stages were very largely substitute, rather than complementary, strategies pursued by two quite different groups of employers. Firstly, we found, contrary to the view of Ross, that definite non-compliance disproportionately occurred in the claims where there had been relatively high levels of employee support for the union; the mean level of support in such cases was 65%, compared to 59% in the cases where agreement had been reached. And secondly, we found, contrary to Prosten, that definite non-compliance characterised the original claims that had taken the least time to be heard and decided. The ballot stage opposition (in the form of procedural delays) was as we have seen, very much a feature of white collar claims in partially unionised, multi-plant establishments. In contrast, correlation analysis revealed that post ballot stage opposition (in the form of non-compliance with the ACAS recommendation) was centred around manual worker claims in small, non-union, single independent establishments. It was these two groups of employers, with their quite different attitudes and strategies, that were identified by ACAS as being most resistant to recognition;(11) their activities largely ensured the non-fulfillment of the earlier identified conditions for the success (from the union point of view) of statutory recognition provisions in an industrial relations system such as Great Britain.

On the complementary/substitution strategy question, there appear to be some differences between our findings for Great Britain and those for the United States. Nevertheless, both procedural delays and ineffective sanctions for non-compliance with recognition recommendations have been identified as problems <u>common</u> to the operation of statutory recognition provisions in both systems of industrial relations. This fact raises the all important question of whether such common problems are in fact <u>inherent</u> ones, essentially incapable of reform. This is a matter that we take up in the following section; the Canadian experience cited in Chapter 2 is also relevant in this regard.

The Response to the Problems of the Provisions

One basic response to these problems was to argue that statutory recognition provisions do not, and cannot, work well in Great Britain in that they do not accord well with the traditions, structures and behaviour patterns of the industrial relations system. This was certainly the position taken by the former chairman of ACAS, Jim Mortimer.(12) The position of ACAS was especially important as the difficulties that it encountered in operating the procedures were undoubtedly influential in the ultimate decision to repeal (through the Employment Act 1980) Sections 11-16 of the Employment Protection Act 1975. In a much publicised letter to the Secretary of State for Employment, the ACAS council high-lighted the following major difficulties that had been encountered with the procedures:(13)

(i)   The Act gave ACAS no guidance on the criteria to be adopted in determining what is an appropriate bargaining unit and the council itself had been unable to agree on any generally applicable criteria;

(ii) some of the specific duties imposed on ACAS by the provisions were not necessarily compatible with its general duty to improve industrial relations;

(iii) where an employer or union refused to co-operate with ACAS, it was left with a duty it could not perform;

(iv) there were potential difficulties in court rulings that ACAS was to be regarded as a tribunal when considering recognition matters;

(v)   the discretion which the council felt is required in order to function properly was seen, as a result of judicial decisions, to be less than was originally envisaged by the Act.

This letter formed the immediate background
to the Department of Employment discussion paper
which preceded the Employment Act 1980, posing the
basic question: 'whether it is necessary or valu-
able to have statutory provisions of this kind to
deal with these matters or whether it would be
better to rely on the ability of ACAS to help
settle recognition disputes through the provision
of voluntary conciliation and advice, as happens
in most cases at present'.(14) This reference to
voluntary conciliation brings us to a second position taken with regard to statutory recognition
provisions. This position is that such provisions
are unnecessary in Great Britain given the existence
of an alternative, and more satisfactory, public
policy based route to recognition, i.e. the
voluntary conciliation facilities provided by ACAS
under the terms of Section 2 of the Employment
Protection Act 1975. This particular view appeared
to be a relatively important factor behind the
General Council of the TUC making a relatively low
profile, non-critical response to the repeal of
Sections 11-16 of the 1975 Act.(15) A third and
final criticism of statutory recognition procedures
stresses their potentially double-edged nature in
the sense of adversely affecting the independence
and character of unions who rely too much on them,
and in terms of opening up the union movement to a
variety of awkward legal quid pro quos that may
constrain them.(16) In the latter case an obvious
possible danger for the unions is alleged to be the
existence of decertifi'cation procedures that permit
the removal of recognition arrangements.
To recapitulate, it has been argued by a
variety of commentators that statutory recognition
provisions (i) cannot work in Britain;(ii) are unnecessary; and (iii) are dangerous to the union
movement. The combination of these three arguments
or beliefs appear to explain why the repeal of the
statutory recognition provisions in 1980 attracted
such little adverse reaction and comment from both
trade unions and industrial relations commentators
in Great Britain. In Chapter 4 we consider the
second of these arguments by examining the use of
voluntary conciliation in recognition claims, while
the potential danger to the unions posed by the quid
pro quo of decertification procedures is considered
in Chapter 6. The remainder of this chapter,
however, takes up the contention that statutory
recognition provisions cannot work in this country
by examining the position in Northern Ireland where

such provisions continue in operation, apparently
with considerable success from the union point of
view.   This situation would appear to constitute
an important challenge to those claiming that such
provisions are inherently incapable of working in
the UK industrial relations environment.   Before
proceeding to an examination of the Northern Ireland
situation, however, we conclude this section by
noting one or two a priori union criticisms of the
view that the problems encountered with statutory
recognition provisions in the years 1976-1980 were
inherent in nature.

One such union was the Engineers and Managers
Association (EMA) which was founded in 1977,
although its parent body (the Electrical Power
Engineers Association) dates back to the early
1930s.   This union is organised in industry based
groups, with the major ones being in electricity
supply, shipbuilding and aerospace.   It has also
secured recognition agreements with individual
firms in engineering, power station construction,
paper and packaging, and the oil industries.   The
EMA is one of the 'open' unions that the Council
of Engineering Institutions recommended as being
suitable for professional engineers, largely on the
grounds of the absence of a political levy and
opposition to the closed shop.   It is not, however,
a party to the national, procedural agreement in
the engineering industry.

On statutory recognition provisions, John Lyons,
the General Secretary of the EMA, outlined his
union's opposition to their repeal in a letter to
The Times of February 13th 1980.   The essence of
his case was that many of the problems experienced
by ACAS with the recognition provisions in the
years 1976-1980 were of their own making;   they
were a result of the way they had chosen to exercise
their discretion in decision making.   Accordingly,
these problems provided, in his view, no case for
repealing the provisions.   Rather, they should have
been strengthened, with employee ballots being made
compulsory in law, and the recommendations also
being made legally binding.   The possibility that
ACAS should not be the body responsible for the
operation of such provisions was also raised.

Various EMA documents indicate that this letter
was not simply a 'one-off' protest.   For example,
representations had been made to the Secretary of
State for Employment in Autumn 1979 opposing the
repeal, a move that obviously bore little success.
The union, however, '... remains convinced that

legislation governing trade union recognition is
necessary in the United Kingdom and it looks to a
future Government to re-introduce such legislation
but improved to prevent the kind of approach taken
by ACAS in relation to the Employment Protection
Act '.(17)

The EMA was certainly not a lone voice crying
in the wilderness at the time of repeal.   There
were also other unions, such as BIFU, opposed to the
repeal of the statutory provisions.   A particularly
interesting union to examine is ASTMS given that,
as we saw earlier, they were one of the early,
leading advocates of such legislation.   Moreover,
they were second only to the TGWU, an organisation
four times their size, in the use of the statutory
provisions in the years 1976-1980, i.e. they put
forward some 265 claims.   A recent study by Sproull,
which sought the views of all ASTMS full-time
officers in Scotland (N = 7) on the subject of
statutory recognition provisions, is most instruc-
tive.(18)   The various officers interviewed
particularly valued statutory provisions as a method
of aiding the recognition process in companies
which (i) denied the union sufficient access to
members;   and (ii) where the members were relatively
new and inexperienced and hence difficult to bring
out through industrial action.   This view makes it
clear that the provisions were valued as a weapon
of last resort, being a useful, if minor (in a
quantitative sense) adjunct to traditional recruitment and recognition tactics.   The benefits of
legal provisions were seen to partly flow from the
positive environment generated, which tended to
encourage voluntary recognition.   All the officers
were unanimously of the opinion that ASTMS had
gained from Sections 11-16 of the Employment Protection Act 1975.   In addition to generating this
positive environmental advantage, all cited claims
that it would have been difficult to win through
any other means.

The officers interviewed cited a number of
perceived weaknesses of the Section 11-16 procedures
which they felt could, and should, be dealt with
in any future legislation.   These included the
absence of a time limit on the length of the procedures, the lack of an obligation on employers to
allow the union(s) access to staff on the premises
in order to counter any anti-union communications,
and the lack of an obligation on employers to
provide information verifying the company's claims
regarding the number of staff on common grades in

multi-plant firms; the latter was viewed as
necessary to try and counter employer tactics of
widening the bargaining unit. And finally, all
pointed to the absence of effective sanctions
against employers who ignored ACAS recommendations
in favour of recognition. The suggested sanctions
included denying such companies regional development grants, regional selective assistance under
Section 7 or sectoral assistance under Section 8 of
the Industry Act 1972, or substantial fines.

When asked to consider the shape of possible
future statutory provisions, all but one of the
ASTMS officers felt that ACAS was the appropriate
third party decision making body. · The one dissent-
ing officer argued that such provisions could, as
with the Section 11-16 ones, pose role conflict
problems for ACAS. All the officers interviewed
felt that ACAS must be given greater powers under
any future legislation. In this regard the major
change they felt to be essential was that ACAS
decisions should be legally binding on the parties
concerned. Some potential difficulties with this
recommendation were acknowledged so that in order
to try and ensure that only limited use had to be
made of compulsory measures an effective code of
practice to encourage voluntary recognition was seen
as essential. The officers were invited to
consider the level of membership necessary in a
potential bargaining unit to use as the basis for
calling a ballot. The responses ranged from around
20 per cent to well over 50 per cent. This variation reflected the sectoral responsibilities of the
officers concerned. At one extreme the officer
for engineering and chemicals reported a below
average reluctance amongst staff to commit themselves to membership prior to recognition and hence
he favoured the 50 per cent plus figure, whereas
the officer responsible for the finance sector was
in favour of 20 per cent as he felt, on the basis of
past experience, that something like 60 per cent
support would follow at the ballot stage. The
officers tended to the view that the result of the
full ballot should be the major determinant of
whether recognition was recommended or not. In
their view discretionary judgements by the third
party body, based on other factors than simply the
level of employee support, would run the serious
risk of conflict with the courts. There was some
disagreement among the officers as to the level of
employee support in the ballot necessary for a

recognition recommendation; some felt that 50 per
cent plus one was necessary to maintain the cred-
ibility and public support of any future legislation, whereas the others felt that 30-40 per cent
was an adequate figure in view of the likely level
of subsequent membership growth.

Finally, a number of the officers talked at
some length of what they saw as an emerging trend
in newly established companies in Scotland to have
staff status arrangements. These companies,
particularly the US ones, were either non-union or
strongly favoured single union recognition agreements. It was in relation to these particular
companies that statutory recognition procedures
were seen to be of particular importance. Moreover, with the companies seeking single union
recognition agreements it was felt that some intervention by the TUC or possibly the STUC might be
necessary to help establish appropriate spheres of
influence in order to avoid, or at least minimise,
the unions competing amongst themselves to the
detriment of individual unions or the movement as a
whole. These latter matters are taken up at some
length in Chapters 4 and 5.

The Northern Ireland Statutory Recognition Provisions

The statutory requirements on trade union recog-
nition, which were established under the Industrial
Relations (Northern Ireland) Order 1976, had their
origins in the Report of the Northern Ireland
Review Body on Industrial Relations (the Quigley
Report) in 1974. When the provisions of the
resulting statutory recognition provisions in
Northern Ireland are compared with those of
Sections 11-16 of the Employment Protection Act
1975, the following differences are apparent:

(i)   The Labour Relations Agency, rather than a
        certification officer, determines whether a
        union is 'independent'.
(ii)   In Northern Ireland employers can refer
        recognition disputes to the Agency.
(iii)   In Northern Ireland the Labour Relations
        Agency can choose to intervene in a recog-
        nition dispute.
(iv)   The definition of recognition is wider in
        Northern Ireland in that a union can be
        recognised for a wider range of subjects,
        including consultation rights.

(v)   The Labour Relations Agency is not obliged
        to inquire into every recognition dispute
        referred to it and, having begun an investi-
        gation, is not obliged to complete it in
        the sense of necessarily making a recommen-
        dation.
(vi)   The Labour Relations Agency is expressly
        permitted to defer its inquiries until
        inter-union dispute machinery has been
        utilised.
(vii)   In the face of employer or union opposition,
        the Labour Relations Agency only has to
        proceed with inquiries to the best of its
        abilities.
(viii) The Agency cannot vary or revoke a recom-
        mendation for recognition after a report of
        failure by the employer to comply with that
        recommendation.
(ix)   A recommendation for recognition becomes
        effective immediately in Northern Ireland.
(x)   A union in Northern Ireland may allege non-
        compliance by an employer immediately,
        rather than having to wait two months as
        was the case in Great Britain.
(xi)   The Agency is not required to attempt to
        conciliate after a non-compliance complaint
        has been made.
(xii)   The Agency determines non-compliance, whereas
        in Great Britain this was done by the CAC
        and not ACAS.

In practice the most important of these differences have been held to be the discretion to
commence and complete inquiries, the express right
to refer disputes to inter-union machinery, and the
absence of the ability to vary or revoke recommendations after a charge of non-compliance has
been made, i.e. numbers (v), (vi) and (viii) above.
(20)   There also exist, or existed, differences
in the administration of the two statutes, with the
most important of these appearing to be the fact
that the Agency, unlike ACAS, made no attempt to
try and develop generally applicable criteria for
determining recognition, and that the Agency,
following acceptance of its recognition recommendations, has sought to assist the parties to
conclude recognition/procedural agreements to
govern their future relationships.

There have certainly been some difficult and
controversial recognition claims for the Agency to
deal with in Northern Ireland.   Perhaps the most

well known of these involved the Irish Saltmining
and Exploration Company, where the Agency was called
in by the union after the workers concerned had
gone on strike and were then dismissed.(21)   The
company refused to co-operate with the Agency in
its inquiries so that the latter was forced to (i)
obtain employees' addresses from the union and
send them postal questionnaires, and (ii) advertise
in the press that Agency staff would be available
in a nearby hotel to hear the views of management
and employees on union recognition.   As a result
of these actions, the Agency was able to obtain the
views of some 70 per cent of employees in the relevant bargaining unit.   The Agency recommended
recognition of the Amalgamated Transport and General
Workers Union, but the company initially refused to
comply with this recommendation and dismissed 24
employees.   However, following the issuance of a
certificate of non-compliance and subsequent
conciliation, the company agreed to recognise the
union and re-engage the dismissed employees with
arrears of pay.

This particular case was exceptional (the
Agency reports only eight other cases of similar
employer non co-operation), and in general commentators are agreed that the statutory provisions
have worked well in Northern Ireland compared to
Great Britain.   The bases of this judgement are
the relatively high proportion of conciliated
settlements, the issuance of few certificates of
non-compliance, the absence of union complaints of
procedural delays and, above all else, the fact
that the provisions have survived and continue to
operate in Northern Ireland at the present time.
There has, however, been some disagreement as to
the major reasons for this success.   In this
matter some have chosen to emphasise the Agency's
greater flexibility as regards its terms of reference and the way it conducts inquiries,(22) while
others have stressed the more harmonious overall
industrial relations climate of Northern Ireland.
(23)   This disagreement is an important matter as
the latter explanation would suggest that a simple
transplant of the Northern Ireland procedures to
Great Britain would not produce similar results.
To date, however, these alternative explanations
have not been subject to any systematic research
or evaluation.   Although we are not in a position
to undertake such a task here, it is certainly
worth noting that the explanation in terms of the
relatively high overall quality of industrial

relations in Northern Ireland tends to argue this
very much in terms of a lower strike frequency than
that of Great Britain.   This seems a most unsatis-
factory basis for such an argument given: (i) the
gap in strike activity between the two has considerably narrowed in recent years(24);   (ii) no single
indicator, such as strike frequency, can adequately
measure a complex, multi-dimensional concept such
as the overall quality of industrial relations;
and (iii) the degree of organised, industrial
conflict would seem to say very little about the
nature of the attitudes and behaviour of employers
in unorganised relationships.   The argument
concerning the importance of the overall quality of
industrial relations may ultimately prove to be the
correct one, but at the present time the nature of
the supporting evidence is certainly inadequate to
the task of proving it.

The first full year of operation of the
provisions in Northern Ireland was 1977/1978 when
20 recognition claims were put forward.   In the
subsequent six years a further 184 claims were
submitted: 22 in 1978/1979;   27 in 1979/1980;
36 in 1980/1981;   34 in 1981/1982;   34 in 1982/1983;
and 31 in 1983/1984.   In short, 204 recognition
claims were received over this seven-year period,
with 182 of these being settled by March 1984.
For the cases settled, the union obtained full
recognition in 51 per cent, partial recognition in
a further 5 per cent and no recognition in the
remaining 44 per cent.

The stages of the procedure at which the 182
cases were settled were as follows:

(i)   By conciliation or advice to the parties,
       without the need for a formal Agency inquiry:
       74%
(ii)   By conciliation after a formal Agency inquiry
       under Article 7 of the order: 15%
(iii) Following issue by the Agency of a report of
       its findings and conclusions to the parties
       in draft form: 4%
(iv)   Following issue by the Agency of a final
       Report containing a definitive recommendation
       under Article 7(i)(d):   4%
(v)   After the issue of a Certificate of Non-
       Compliance to the trade union concerned: 3%

This small absolute number of recognition claims needs to be seen in the context of an industrial relations system with a relatively high base level of union organisation, a level estimated to be somewhat higher in fact than that in Great Britain.(25)

The remainder of this chapter considers the outcomes of 143 recognition claims heard and decided during the first six years of operation of the provisions. The fact that 30 of the total number of 173 claims heard in these years were missing was simply due to their relevant details being not recorded, a reason which gives us little cause to believe that our resulting analysis may be biased. The outcome of our 143 recognition claims was as follows: full recognition in 45 per cent; partial recognition in another 6 per cent; and no recognition in the remaining 49 per cent of claims. An examination of the size of the bargaining unit in each claim where a union achieved full or partial recognition revealed that 3,487 employees were brought under collective bargaining coverage and a further 1,086 received partial coverage. These figures may, however, overstate the contribution of the recognition provisions to increased union membership for two basic reasons. First, these figures are for collective bargaining coverage which, as we have already seen, is not synonymous with union membership. And secondly, as we have again seen, the extent of employer non-compliance with recommendations for union recognition may be considerably in excess of that suggested by a simple head count of the number of union complaints of such non-compliance. Unfortunately, we have no Northern Ireland specific sources of information on these two matters which would allow us to make the necessary adjustments to the above figures in order to calculate the number of trade union members that resulted from the operation of the provisions. Moreover, the absence of systematic and comprehensive figures for total trade union membership in Northern Ireland for individual years effectively precludes us from making any attempt to estimate the proportionate contribution of the provisions to total union membership growth in the years 1977-1983.

The basic characteristics of our 143 recognition claims are set out below in Table 3.3.

Statutory Recognition Provisions

Table 3.3   Characteristics of the Northern Ireland
            Recognition Claims, 1977/78 - 1982/83

Manufacturing sector	44%
Three major union users (TGWU, Irish Transport and General Workers Union, APEX)	51%
White collar	42%
Multi-union claims	20%
Mean bargaining unit size	148
Mean length of time involved	7.9 months
Non-union establishments	75%
Conciliated claims	85%

Source: P.B. Beaumont, 'Trade Union Recognition
        in Northern Ireland', British Journal of
        Industrial Relations, Vol.22, No.3,
        November 1984.

The variable of particular interest to us here is that of non-union status as this is utilised here as a new, potential measure of the extent of employer opposition to recognition.   The rationale for its use in this regard is provided by US studies that have suggested that management's desire to avoid further unionisation is very much a function of the level of existing workforce unionisation,(26) i.e. the lower the level of existing workforce organisation, the greater the desire or priority attached by management to avoiding further organisation.   And, almost by definition, this management desire should be greatest in a non-union plant. Accordingly, we hypothesise that in non-union, as opposed to partially unionised, plants there will be a principled employer opposition to recognition which is likely to be associated with a lower likelihood of a union receiving a third party recommendation for recognition.   The performance of this variable will be compared with that of our previous measure of such opposition, namely the length of time involved in hearing and deciding the claim.

The correlation coefficients between unions obtaining full recognition and these two variables, as well as the others listed in Table 3.3, are set out below in Table 3.4.   This analysis was only conducted on the number of claims where information

for all of the independent variables was recorded,
(N =132).

Table 3.4: Correlations Between Full Recognition
            and Independent Variables

Non-union status	0.199 **
Duration of claim	-0.190 **
Service industries	0.096
Conciliated settlement	-0.023
Major union users	-0.012
Multi-union claim	-0.243 **
White collar bargaining group	0.047
Size of bargaining group	-0.147 *

* = significant at the .10 level
** = significant at the .05 level

Source; Beaumont, Loc.cit.

The contents of Table 3.4 indicate that 4 of
our 8 variables are statistically significant,
namely non-union status, the length of time taken
to hear and decide the claim, multi-union claims
and the size of the bargaining unit.   In line with
the results of Table 3.2 we find that full recognition was less likely to be achieved in multi-
union claims, in larger sized bargaining units and
in claims which took a relatively long time to hear
and decide.   Our new variable, non-union status,
was also significant, but it entered with the
opposite sign to that predicted.   That is, our
results show that full recognition was more (and
not less) likely to be achieved in claims involving
non-union plants.   This finding means that either
non-union status is not a useful proxy for initial
and sustained employer opposition to union recognition, or that it is, but that the unions have
successfully responded to and overcome this opposition.
     In order to try and distinguish between these
two possible interpretations we firstly examined
the relationship between non-union status and our
traditional employer opposition proxy, the length
of time taken to hear and decide the claim.   They

were significantly, but negatively, correlated
(r = -0.256), indicating that those claims in non-
union plants took a significantly shorter length
of time to be heard and decided.   The nature of
this relationship certainly casts strong doubts on
any notion that the non-union plant claims involved
sustained employer opposition to recognition.   As
a further test, we computed the correlation coefficients between these two proxies for employer
opposition and the rest of our variables.   The
results are set out in Table 3.5.

Table 3.5:   Correlation Between (i) Duration
              of Claim and (ii) Non-Union Status
              and Other Variables

	(i) Duration of claim	(ii) Non-Union Status
Service industries	0.154 *	-0.166 *
Conciliated settlement	-0.454 ***	0.232 ***
Major union users	-0.238 ***	0.294 ***
Multi-union status	0.346 ***	-0.639 ***
White collar bargaining group	0.130	-0.046
Size of bargaining group	0.206 **	-0.278 ***

*   = significant at the .10 level
** = significant at the .05 level
*** = significant at the .01 level

Source: Beaumont, Loc.cit.

_____

The same 5 variables are statistically significant, but in all cases they have different signs,
thus indicating that the associated characteristics
of these two alleged proxies for employer opposition to recognition are really quite different.
The length of time taken to hear and decide claims
was relatively long in multi-union claims, in claims
with a relatively sizeable bargaining unit, and in
claims in the service industries, whereas it was
significantly shorter in claims where there had
been a conciliated settlement and in claims
involving the major union users.

In the case of non-union plant status we find that these claims were less likely to be multi-union ones, involved relatively small sized bargaining units, were less likely to be in the service industries, but were more likely to be conciliated and more likely to involve the major union users. The latter variable might suggest that non-union status was proxying employer opposition, but that this opposition was successfully overcome by the three unions highly committed to recruitment and organisational expansion. However, on balance we think it unlikely that this non-union variable can be treated as a satisfactory proxy for such opposition given that these claims were so much more likely to be conciliated and, as previously noted, took a relatively short time to be heard and decided. In stating this view we acknowledge the possibility that an initial strong employer opposition in these claims may have declined once it became apparent, perhaps at the employers' insistence, that it was to be single union recognition involving only a relatively small sized bargaining group. These favourable (and possibly sought after) factors from the employer point of view may have caused any initial strong employer opposition to have declined relatively quickly. In short, non-union status may, at best, have proxied an initial employer opposition to recognition, but it does not appear to have captured the influence of sustained opposition.

These 'negative' interpretations of non-union plant status as a proxy for employer opposition bring us back to the question of the value of the traditional proxy for such opposition, namely the length of time taken to hear and decide a claim. As with previous research, we find that the longer the time involved in a claim the less likely the union is to win. Moreover, a number of the associated characteristics of relatively long duration claims, such as the disproportionate concentration in the little organised service industries, the low likelihood of conciliation, the relatively sizeable bargaining units and the fact of multi-union claims, would all seem reasonably consistent with the interpretation that relatively long duration claims involve the presence of substantial and sustained employer opposition to recognition. In short, although we certainly need to know more about the factors involved in relatively long duration claims, it would appear that, in the absence of more unambiguous alternative measures or proxies, this particular factor is probably our most useful proxy, at least at the present time, for the extent of employer opposition to recognition.

Conclusions

The union win rate under the still operational statutory procedures in Northern Ireland appears to be most impressive when compared with that achieved in Great Britain under Sections 11-16 of the Employment Protection Act 1975. This apparent outcome difference brings us back to the question of the relative importance, as explanatory factors, of differences in the two statutes (and associated administrative arrangements), as opposed to differences in the quality of the overall industrial relations climate. This question obviously awaits future study. At the present moment, however, the continued operation of statutory recognition provisions in Northern Ireland must pose a considerable challenge to the view that such provisions cannot hope to work properly in the UK context. This is a matter returned to in the concluding chapter.

The other conclusion to be emphasised here is the extent of similarity with some of the findings in the United States that were considered in Chapter 2. This review of statutory recognition provisions indicates the considerable management opposition to union attempts to achieve recognition for previously unorganised bargaining units, with this opposition occurring at both the ballot and post ballot stages. The former was particularly associated with white collar claims in partially unionised establishments, while the latter tended to occur more in small, single independent establishments that were non-union. The continued extent of such opposition is considered in Chapter 4, while Chapter 5 explores some of the factors that may stimulate such opposition, at least among the latter group of establishments.

NOTES

1. R. Price and G.S. Bain, "Union Growth Revisited: 1948-1974 in Perspective", British Journal of Industrial Relations, Vol.14, No.3, November 1976, pp.341-344.

2. B. Weekes et al, Industrial Relations and the Limits of the Law, Basil Blackwell, Oxford, 1975, pp.131-147.

3.   B. James, "Third Party Intervention in Recognition Disputes: The Role of the Commission on Industrial Relations", Industrial Relations Journal, Vol.8, No.2, Summer 1977, p.39.

4.   ACAS Annual Report 1980, HMSO, London, 1981 p.99.

5.   ACAS Annual Report, 1980, Loc.cit.

6.   Clive Jenkins and Barrie Sherman, White Collar Unionism, Routledge and Kegan Paul, London, 1979, p.98.

7.   ACAS Annual Report 1980, ibid., p.83.

8.   B. Doyle, "A Substitute for Collective Bargaining? The Central Arbitration Committee's Approach to Section 16 of the Employment Protection Act 1975", Industrial Law Journal, Vol.9, 1980, p.165.

9.   Annual Report of the Central Arbitration Committee 1980, HMSO, London.

10.   T.A. Kochan, Collective Bargaining and Industrial Relations, Irwin, Homewood, 1980, p.187.

11.   ACAS Annual Report, 1980, ibid., p.90.

12.   J. Mortimer, "ACAS and the Development of Collective Bargaining", Personnel Management, March 1981, p.38.

13.   ACAS Annual Report 1980, ibid., pp.134-138.

14.   Department of Employment Gazette, September 1979, p.874.

15.   Annual Report of the TUC, 1982, p.30.

16.   Moira Hart, "Union Recognition in America - the Legislative Snare", Industrial Law Journal, Vol.7, 1978, p.215.

17.   The EMA Consolidates, 1979-1981, Report to Biannual Delegate Conference by the General Executive Council, p.5.

18.   Alan C. Sproull, "Trade Union Recruitment and the Law: the ASTMS Experience", Unpublished M.Phil in Industrial Relations Dissertation, University of Glasgow, 1983.

19.   Robert Knowlton Sholl, "An Analysis of Northern Ireland Statutory Trade Union Recognition Procedure", Unpublished M.A. Dissertation, University of Warwick, 1980, Chapter 5.

20.   Sholl, ibid., p.12 (Chapter 5)

21.   See Industrial Relations Review and Report, No.214, December 1979, pp.12-13.

22.   Industrial Relations Review and Report, Loc.cit.

23.   Sholl, ibid., pp.14-18 (Chapter 5).

24.   Boyd Black, "Industrial Relations in
Northern Ireland: A Survey", _Industrial Relations
Journal_, Vol.15, No.1, Spring 1984, p.32.
    25.   Boyd Black, _Loc.cit._
    26.   See, for example, Kochan, _op.cit._,
pp.187-189.

Chapter Four

CONCILIATION AND VOLUNTARY INITIATIVES FOR
RECOGNITION

In the previous chapter we introduced an argument
to the effect that statutory recognition provisions
were unnecessary in Great Britain because of the
existence of an alternative, and more satisfactory,
public policy based route to recognition.   This
alternative route being the voluntary conciliation
facilities provided by ACAS under the terms of
Section 2 of the Employment Protection Act 1975.
The current validity or basis of this argument is
now examined; it is perhaps worth noting here that
in Northern Ireland there have been no two such
separate routes to recognition.
      Voluntary conciliation over matters in dispute
between unions and management has, of course, been
a widely accepted feature of the industrial relations system in Britain, for almost a century.   The
basic role of the conciliator is to clarify the
areas of agreement and disagreement between the
parties, act as an intermediary in the exchange of
information and proposals, and to suggest approaches
to a settlement.   It would appear that trade union
recognition issues have figured prominently in the
workload of the responsible conciliation bodies at
particular points in time.   For instance, in the
three years 1970-1972 some 31% of conciliation cases
handled by the Department of Employment involved
trade union recognition claims, a figure only
exceeded by disputes over wages questions (i.e.
38%).(1)   Moreover, the particular appeal of
conciliation in recognition disputes has been well
documented in surveys of trade union officials.(2)
However, despite such figures and findings, there
have always been certain reservations expressed
about the ability of the conciliation method to
deal satisfactorily with trade union recognition
claims.   The sort of reservations expressed are
88

typified by the following extract from the written
evidence of the Ministry of Labour to the Donovan
Commission:(3)

> There may be no common ground as to the facts
> about trade union membership which can, there-
> fore, only be ascertained by thorough and
> independent investigation.   Also on a recog-
> nition issue a conciliator who is seeking a
> basis for settlement cannot in practice take
> up a neutral position between the parties.
> He is bound to appear to the employer as an
> agent for the trade union.   On general grounds
> this is undesirable.

This sort of view, which is certainly consistent with the findings of US studies regarding
the difficulties of conciliation (mediation) in
dealing with 'disputes of principle' in industrial
relations,(4) was in fact part of the case made for
setting up an independent tribunal to hear and
recommend on union recognition claims brought under
statutory provisions.(5)   Nevertheless, during
the years 1976-1980 there were more recognition
claims heard (i.e. 2,290), and with a higher union
win rate (i.e. 43%), under voluntary conciliation
than under the statutory provisions.(6)   There
were some 77,500 employees brought under collective
agreement coverage by the former means which, when
adjusted on the same basis as in the previous
chapter, suggests that voluntary conciliation
accounted for some 11% of the total trade union
membership increase in the years 1976-1980.

The Current Conciliation Position

The union optimism and faith in voluntary conciliation that derived from these figures did, however,
assume the essential independence of operation of
the two public policy based routes for obtaining
recognition in the years 1976-1980, and does, of
course, predate the full onset of the current
recession.   The question examined here is what
has happened to union claims for recognition under
voluntary conciliation since the repeal of the
statutory provisions, and the substantial rise in
unemployment in Great Britain.   The first set of
evidence on this question is for the total number
of recognition claims heard under voluntary conciliation in Great Britain in the years 1976-1984.
These figures are set out below in Table 4.1.

Table 4.1:   Section 2 Recognition Claims,
             Great Britain, 1976-1984

Year	Number of completed conciliation cases concerned with recognition	Recognition claims as a percentage of all completed conciliation cases
1976	697	24
1977	635	22
1978	451	17
1979	392	17
1980	329	17
1981	247	14
1982	232	14
1983	216	13
1984	221	15

Source: Relevant ACAS Annual Reports, HMSO,
          London.

With the repeal of the statutory provisions in 1980, one might have expected, ceteris paribus, that the number of recognition claims would in fact increase under Section 2, this now being the only public policy based route to recognition in Great Britain.   However, not everything else has remained constant, and with the economic recession there has been a very substantial fall in the absolute number of recognition claims since 1980.   The proportion of conciliation cases involving recognition has also fallen, although the extent of this fall needs to be seen in the context of a fall in the total number of conciliation cases over this period of time.

At the national level we lack detailed, year to year information on the outcome of these recognition claims, at least since 1980;   the ACAS annual report for 1983 did, however, suggest a union win rate of some 40% in 1980-1982.(7)   This information is, however, available for a single ACAS region, namely Scotland, which typically handles around 10% of the total conciliation workload of the service.   The basic results from this particular source of information are set out in Table 4.2 below.

Table 4.2:   The Number and Outcome of Recognition
             Claims, ACAS Scotland, 1976-1984

Year	Number of claims	% of total claims	Union win rate (i.e. full recognition) for the year	% of all union win claims
1976	80	20	41	24
1977	68	17	40	19
1978	68	17	47	23
1979	48	12	33	12
1980	34	9	24	6
1981	24	6	21	4
1982	14	4	14	1
1983	23	6	27	4
1984	43	11	23	7

Source: P.B. Beaumont, 'Trade Union Recognition
          and the Recession in the UK ', Industrial
          Relations Journal, Vol.16, No.2, Summer
          1985.

The contents of Table 4.2 indicate that both
the number of recognition claims, and those where
the unions were successful, were disproportionately
concentrated in the years 1976-1980.   These five
years witnessed fully 75% of all claims, and 84% of
all claims where the unions achieved full recognition.   There would appear to be three possible
explanations, which are certainly not mutually
exclusive, of the fall in the number of successful
(from the union point of view) recognition claims
in recent years.   These are as follows:

(i)   the substantial rise in unemployment from
1979 which is likely to have significantly reduced
the inclination and willingness of employers to
seriously discuss the question of trade union recognition.   (The other side of the coin is that the
trade unions are quite likely to have reduced the
priority attached to the obtaining of new recognition agreements given the myriad of other problems
that they face as a result of the recession.)
This is likely to be the major factor responsible
for the falling number of claims apparent in
Table 4.2, although whether it is of such importance
in accounting for the falling union win rate is

rather more debatable. Unfortunately, the lack of comparable data for other ACAS regions rules out the possibility of our seeing whether the union win rate has systematically varied according to regional unemployment levels, etc.

(ii) The repeal of the statutory recognition provisions in 1980 is potentially important in explaining the fall in the union win rate. This is because of the perception and use by the unions of the statutory provisions as a 'last resort' measure whereby a disproportionate number of difficult cases were taken through this route (in this regard it is worth noting that at least some 24% of the unsuccessful, Section 2 claims in Scotland in 1976-1980 were then taken by the unions through the statutory provisions route). Accordingly, with their repeal, such claims can now only be taken through the voluntary conciliation route. This particular effect could be indicated by the existence of significant compositional differences in the recognition claims of the pre- and post-1980 years. Some evidence on this matter is presented below.

(iii) The repeal of the statutory provisions could also have adversely affected the union win rate under voluntary conciliation in another possible way. This is through their absence as a background influence or stimulus which previously allowed ACAS conciliation officers to stress to employers the relative advantage of seriously discussing union recognition claims under voluntary conciliation, and thereby avoiding possible entanglement in the statutory provisions where their capacity to satisfactorily shape the details of any resulting arrangement may have been somewhat less. A specific illustration is provided below in order to indicate the sort of consequences that may have resulted from the removal of this potential 'interdependence' effect.

As regards hypothesis (ii) above, we firstly constructed and tested a 'bargaining unit characteristics' model of the determinants of union success in these recognition claims; the model utilised had considerable similarities to that utilised in the analysis of Chapter 3. The full 402 claims that constituted the basis of Table 4.2 were examined and our independent variables (with their expected relationship to union success indicated in parentheses) were as follows: the three unions most involved in bringing claims (+); manufacturing sector claims (+); multi-plant status (+); the size of the bargaining unit (-); industrial action threatened or took place (-); the length of time involved in hearing and deciding the claim (-); a manual claim (+); and a dummy variable differentiating the post 1980 claims (-).

The results of correlation and multiple regression analysis revealed that only the latter variable was statistically significant, indicating that claims referred post-1980 were less likely to result in full recognition occurring. From the analytical point of view, it is clear that this type of bargaining unit characteristics model has much less explanatory and predictive power when examining the outcome of claims heard under voluntary conciliation, compared with that under statutory recognition, arrangements. The model did enjoy somewhat more success for the sub-period 1976-1980 where it was found that the longer the time involved in hearing and deciding claims (as a proxy for the extent of employer opposition), the less likely the union was to achieve full recognition; the length of time involved was itself positively associated with large sized bargaining units and service sector claims.

The post-1980 claims were significantly characterised by (i) a relatively high proportion of manual claims; (ii) a relatively high proportion of single plant claims; and (iii) a relatively short period of time in which claims were heard and decided. These findings indicate that there were indeed compositional differences between the pre- and post-1980 recognition claims. However, on the basis of our existing evidence, we would have expected these compositional changes to have generally worked in favour of raising the union win rate in the post-1980 period; something that has clearly not occurred. For example, as we have continually stressed, all the available evidence indicates that the longer the time taken to hear and decide a claim, the less likely the union is to win it. However, in the post-1980 claims the average length of time involved (i.e. 1.5 calendar months) was shorter than in the pre-1980 claims (i.e. 2.1 calendar months). Admittedly, the increased proportion of single, independent establishments in the post-1980 period may have involved stronger employer opposition to recognition, but the other two associated characteristics would seem to suggest, at least on conventional interpretations,

a reduction in the extent of such opposition.
Accordingly, our findings do not appear to lend any
obvious and strong support for the influence of
hypothesis (ii) in accounting for the reduced union
win rate of recent years.

The influence of hypothesis (iii) is extremely
difficult to test on any comprehensive and systematic basis.   However, some evidence for its existence is suggested by the details of the specific
illustration outlined below.   This particular
example was obtained from a union that has, through
experience, become increasingly concerned with the
limited 'clout' of voluntary conciliation arrangements for hearing recognition claims in the absence
of statutory provisions in the background.

This example (which did not occur in Scotland)
concerns a particular building society where a
ballot was held on the matter of transferring
engagements from a staff association to the Banking,
Insurance and Finance Union (BIFU).   The ballot,
which was held in early 1984 under the auspices of
the Electoral Reform Society, produced an 84% turnout rate with the following results: in favour of
a transfer to BIFU 96% (N = 162); against a transfer to BIFU 4% (N = 6). \ Following these results
BIFU wrote to the building society requesting a
meeting to discuss recognition, a request that was
rejected on the grounds that (i) the membership of
the staff association had declined significantly
in recent years, and that the staff association
therefore no longer represented the majority of
staff within the society, and (ii) there is no
evidence that the majority of staff wish to be
represented by BIFU.   In addition to this response,
the building society informed the staff association
of their decision to withdraw immediately from the
recognition and procedure agreement.   The consequences of this action were as follows:

(i)   the society no longer recognised the staff
        association for collective bargaining or
        consultation purposes, nor in respect of
        representational rights;
(ii)   the use of the internal mail system, notice
        boards and office accommodation were with-
        drawn as facilities by the society to the
        staff association;
(iii)   check-off facilities were withdrawn;

(iv)   staff association officials were no longer
          allowed time off work for association
          business, nor were association meetings
          to be permitted during working hours.

     BIFU then sought the assistance of ACAS in
this matter.   The building society indicated to
ACAS that membership of the staff association had
fallen from approximately 60% of the bargaining
unit in 1974, when recognition was first granted,
to approximately 32% at the time of the ballot.
In subsequent weeks, BIFU raised their membership
to around 60% of the society's employees and then
contacted ACAS again who, in turn, met the building
society.   ACAS raised the possibility of conducting
a ballot of all staff on the recognition issue
suggesting that the society and BIFU should mutually
agree the terms of the questions to be asked in the
ballot and the level of support necessary for recognition to be granted.   This proposal was rejected
by the building society.
     Following this impasse, BIFU suggested to
their members in the society that a petition should
be circulated calling on the society to recognise
BIFU for the purposes of collective bargaining.
Individual members expressed concern about this
proposal, fearing an adverse management reaction.
However, more than 50% of the potential bargaining
unit have signed the petition to date.   This sort
of experience was obviously a major factor behind
BIFU's successful motion at the Annual Meeting of
the TUC in 1984;   a motion that expressed considerable reservations about the effectiveness of
voluntary conciliation arrangements for dealing
with recognition claims in the current economic
and industrial relations climate.   A fuller indication of current recognition initiatives by BIFU
in the finance sector is contained in the next
section.   However, as background for this present-
ation we conclude this section by providing some
evidence on the numerical importance of public
policy, as opposed to voluntary, based initiatives
for recognition.
     This evidence, which comes from the 1980
DE/SSRC/PSI workplace industrial relations survey,
concerns sizeable white collar bargaining groups
that were covered by written recognition agreements
during the years 1975-1980.   The means by which
recognition was obtained for these 238 bargaining
units was as follows:

(i)   with ACAS involvement (overwhelmingly
        conciliation)   3.3%
(ii)   through union-management discussions 76.5%
(iii)   through recognition being extended   11.3%
(iv)   through an employee ballot   8.8%

The obvious point to make here concerns the
numerical preponderance of recognition obtained
through voluntary means.   ACAS was only directly
involved in some 3% of cases, although its indirect
influence may have been rather greater due to
possibly stimulating a wider use of employee
ballots, a technique that was extensively used in
the services investigations of recognition claims.
These figures should be borne in mind when considering the subsequent discussion of voluntary (and
public policy) initiatives for recognition.   They
could also, hopefully, be the basis of some useful
future research in that it would be interesting to
see whether the establishments that made use of
ACAS (or employee ballots) in recognition claims
had certain identifiable organisational characteristics in common that distinguished them from those
where recognition was obtained through discussion
or extension.   Through such an exercise one might
be able to highlight some of the relevant factors
thatunderlie Daniel and Millward's intuitively
appealing, if untested, comment that 'the places
where ... balloting was carried out or where ACAS
was called in may well have been more important
than they were common, as they may have created
precedents, generated expectations and so on'.(8)

Voluntary Recognition Initiatives in the
Finance Sector

The substantive discussion of this section needs to
be seen in the larger context of the traditional
trade union approach to recruitment and recognition
in the UK.   The first point to note here is that a
union like BIFU is rather unusual in having specialist recruitment officers, as the more common
approach is to '... take a more reactive approach
and wait for potential members to come before
setting a campaign in operation'.(9)This observation
is clearly consistent with Bains'finding that only
three out of the 60 white collar union officials
he interviewed claimed to spend more than 10% of
their time on recruitment activities.(10)   This
essentially reactive posture has been seen to be
supported by Bains'work which has questioned the
value and success of any special recruitment drives

that have occurred.   Indeed Bain, in considering
the determinants of white collar union density in
the workforce as a whole, is very much of the view
that the really influential determinants are those
of the external environment, and as such largely
lie outside the control of individual unions.

This general view has been challenged by the
authors of a recent study of a number of individual
unions.(11)   Their findings lead them to conclude
that individual unions that were positively orientated towards recruitment (through a variety of
actions such as enhancing their image, promoting
recruitment campaigns and providing more local
recruiting agents) achieved membership increases
for themselves which were not at the expense of
other unions, and therefore contributed to an overall union membership increase in the years under
investigation.   This debate or controversy may be
more apparent than real, with the individuals
concerned talking past each other.   In this regard
one needs to take account of the fact that, firstly,
Undy et al are talking about union membership, and
not union density which was the concern of Bain.
And, secondly, the level of aggregation of the
analysis was very different between the two studies,
one being concerned with the individual union level
and the other with the white collar employment
sector as a whole;   differences in levels of
organisational analysis inevitably result in
different emphases on the question of the degree
of choice or discretion available to the actors in
any system.(12)

The finance sector is an excellent context in
which to consider these two points in a little more
detail.   This is because Robert Taylor (writing
originally in 1978) felt that 'over the next few
years BIFU may find it hard to grow rapidly',(13)
and yet now it would appear that BIFU is the fastest
growing union in the UK.   As an illustration of
the latter point, consider the figures set out
below in Table 4.3.

Table 4.3:   Percentage Membership Change for
              Selected Individual Unions, 1979-1982

Union	Change
TGWU	-17.9%
AUEW(Eng)	-15.0%
GMWU	-10.3%
NALGO	+ 9.1%
NUPE	- 1.1%
ASTMS	- 9.1%
EETPU	- 5.9%
NUT	-23.0%
CPSA	- 6.25%
AUEW(TASS)	- 7.5%
NUR	-12.2%
BIFU	+17.5%

Source: The Economist, 11th September 1982

The relative success of BIFU is clear, with
NALGO being the only other union in the Table to
record an increase in membership for these years.
Indeed taking BIFU over the years 1979-1984 we find
that membership appears to have increased by
between 20 and 25%.   A rule change in 1971 permitted BIFU (formerly NUBE) to recruit members outwith the banking industry.   This change, which was
estimated to have raised its potential membership
from some 200,000 to around 500,000 (14), permitted
BIFU to broaden its approach of 'growth by merger',
with the Royal Bank of Scotland Staff Association
being absorbed in 1975, the Guardian Royal Exchange
Staff Union in 1978 and the Phoenix Staff Union in
1979.   It is,nevertheless,a well accepted dictum
that unions tend invariably to concentrate their
recruitment activities on familiar ground, i.e. they
will continue to recruit in well established areas
of relatively little resistance.   This suggests
that much of the BIFU membership increase in the
post-1979 years is likely to have occurred in
banking.
    According to at least one study, this has
certainly been the case.(15)   The reasons for this
disproportionate concentration are the relatively
favourable employer attitudes in banking compared
to the rest of the finance sector.   These relatively favourable attitudes have been manifested
in a number of ways.   For example, the terms of
the procedural agreements signed with the English

and Scottish banks ensure that the full-time
officers of BIFU can have relatively easy access
to employees for recruitment purposes, the union
has involvement rights in the training programmes
for new employees and more than 80% of membership
in the banking sector is on the check-off system.
In order to capitalise on these advantages BIFU has
taken a number of 'growth orientated decisions'
which are similar to some of the examples cited in
the Undy et al study referred to earlier.   For
example, in response to the growth in part-time
employment in the banks since 1980 BIFU has reduced
their subscription for part-time employees; the
result was a significant increase in part-time
membership in 1980-1982.   Secondly, recent use has
been made of temporary recruiting agents for short,
intensive periods of time in the clearing banks;
the 12-week English clearing bank campaign in 1984
saw particular use made of such individuals.
These sorts of initiatives have been taken through
the National Membership Committee of BIFU which is
responsible for devising, implementing and monitor-
ing recruitment strategies; the existence of such
a specialist, national level body for recruitment
purposes, backed up by a full-time organising staff,
is relatively unusual among British trade unions.
    This combination of receptive employer atti-
tudes and growth orientated initiatives should not
lead one to believe that BIFU's record of membership
recruitment in banking has been an unmixed success
story in recent years.   The other side of the coin
has seen management initiated changes in the terms
of procedural agreements, largely involving the
removal of the unilateral right to arbitration.
In addition, the movement of certain banks into the
financial securities industry appears to be associated with attempts to ensure non-union status.
Barclays, for example, are reported to have transferred some 300 staff from their merchant bank into
a new investment subsidiary, Barclays De Zoete Wedd,
where unions will not be recognised; Lloyds have
also set up a merchant bank where unions are not
recognised.(16)   And finally, and most importantly
in view of our earlier discussion of the Bain -v-
Undy et al debate, the substantially increased
membership of BIFU in the banking sector has not
meant anything like a comparable sized increase
in the level of union density (associated with this
particular union).   The competition of the three
non-TUC affiliated Staff Associations (Barclays,

Lloyds and National Westminster) that form the
Clearing Bank Union continues (despite periodic
discussions between them and BIFU since 1980 on the
subject of merger), with the CBU organising margin-
ally more staff than BIFU in the English clearing
banks.   This competition in the context of an
increase in overall employment numbers has meant,
according to some unpublished calculations prepared
by Peter Cressey (University of Glasgow), that the
union density associated with BIFU in the clearing
banks has increased very much less than their
membership increase there since 1979.

BIFU's own estimates are that employment
numbers in the banking area will decline in the
next 5 - 10 years, largely as a result of the impact
of new technology.   For this reason alone there
will have to be increased attention paid to
membership recruitment in the rest of the finance
sector.   This point has not escaped a number of
other unions.   For example, ASTMS announced in 1983
its willingness to conclude 'association agreements'
with staff associations in the finance sector.
These agreements are seen as a means of enabling
potential merger partners to gain an appreciation of
the benefits that would result from merger.   The
first such agreement has been concluded for a 2 year
period with the 5,000-member Sun Alliance Staff
Association.   During this time the association pays
ASTMS a fee and has agreed not to discuss with any
other union the possibility of a merger; in return,
ASTMS cannot mount an active recruitment campaign
in Sun Alliance during this time.   In return for
the fee, the Sun Alliance Staff Association obtains
access to various ASTMS services and facilities,
most notably those of education, training and
information and advice from the research, health
and safety, and legal departments of the union.

One particular part of the finance sector
where unions like BIFU are keen to make membership
inroads is the building societies.   This is,
however, likely to be a far from easy task given
the well documented attitudes of opposition (to
employees being represented by external bodies)
held by the senior management of many building
societies.(17)   In the early 1970s BIFU was able
to obtain procedural agreements with some 8 or 9
smaller building societies, with at least one of
these being a legally binding agreement that
involved sole negotiating rights in return for a no-
strike clause and arbitration arrangements.(18)

In the subsequent 10 years or so BIFU has been able
to add little to this total number of procedural
agreements with building societies.   In contrast,
there has been a very considerable growth of staff
associations in building societies over the same
period of time.   There were some 7 staff associations in 1974, but by 1982 this number had grown
to 23, with nearly 50% of these having come into
existence since 1979.(19)   Moreover, many of these
associations would appear to have relatively high
membership density figures.   This fact is illustrated by the contents of Table 4.4.

    Although only 23 out of the 250 building
societies (at the beginning of 1982) had staff
associations, these arrangements appear to be
disproportionately associated with the larger
societies; the importance of this relationship
follows from the merger trends in the industry (at
the end of 1984 there were only 190 registered
building societies in Great Britain).   By the end
of 1982 13 of the 23 staff associations listed in
Table 4.4 had applied for and obtained certificates
of independence.   This fact suggested that an
important change in the legal (and associated
administrative) environment since 1974 has provided
the management of building societies with an increased capacity to minimise the external representation of employees through the substitution of
internal representation arrangements; this is an
excellent example of an environmental change
enhancing the capacity of employers to operate on
a non-union basis (see Chapter 1).   A number of
individual trade union leaders have been highly
critical of the relative ease with which staff
associations now appear able to obtain certificates
of independence relative to the years 1971-1974.
At the Annual Meeting of the TUC in 1976, for
example, the speaker for BIFU (or as it then was
NUBE) proposed the following changes to the system
of granting certificates of independence:(20)

(i)   The Act should provide for the definition (of
       independence) to include matters such as
       effectiveness, resources, history and the
       industrial relations impact of the bodies;
(ii)   ACAS, rather than the certification officer,
       should make the decision as they can take
       account of the wider context of the applicant
       organisation;

Table 4.4: Building Society Associations,
Employment and Membership 1980

Building Society	Numbers Employed	Number in Staff Association	Density (%)
Abbey National	7,606	5,549	73
Anglia	2,017	1,161	58
Bradford and Bingley	1,642	1,120	68
Burnley	1,014	822	81
Chelsea	330	258	78
Cheshire	235	153	65
Coventry Economic	356	220	62
Derbyshire	390	267	69
Gateway	788	652	83
Halifax	9,272	7,984	86
Huddersfield and Bradford*	807	673	83
Leek and Westbourne**	1,229	1,004	82
Leicester	1,874	1,338	71
Midshires	465	316	68
Nationwide	3,977	2,933	74
Northern Rock	746	524	70
Portman	263	192	73
Provincial	1,756	1,448	83
Staffordshire	277	223	81
Sussex County	174	126	72
Town and County	406	292	72
West Bromwich	391	221	57
Woolwich	2,519	1,839	73

Notes: *Since 1 January 1982 West Yorkshire
Building Society
**Merged with Britannia Building Society 1979

Source: A.I.R. Swabe and Patricia Price 'Building
a Permanent Association? The Development
of Staff Associations in the Building
Societies', British Journal of Industrial
Relations, Vol.22, No.2, July 1984, p.196.

(iii) existing issues of certificates should
be revoked as soon as the necessary legal
amendment is carried through;

(iv) and finally, and most importantly, the
acid test of a staff association being
independent is whether it would have survived
or existed at all without recognition from
the employer.

This motion (condemning the ease with which
certificates of independence were obtained by
staff associations) was carried, although the
General Council representative stressed the likelihood of considerable difficulties being associated with its implementation; the particular fear
expressed was that the tighter the registration/
certification requirements, the more one moved
towards a system of state licensing of trade unions
with its potential adverse consequences for TUC
affiliated unions.

Following a survey of some 88 staff associations the certification officer observed that
'although such organisations can operate at low
cost, with subscription rates far below those of
competing unions, they are poorly protected against
unexpected hostility from a previously benevolent
employer';(21) recall here the example cited
earlier in this chapter of a unilateral withdrawal
from a procedural agreement. From the late 1970s
the certification officer has allowed more opportunity for union representations against a staff
association application for a certificate of independence. Moreover, in the appeals concerning
Squabb UK Staff Association, the Court of Appeal
supported the position of the certification officer,
as opposed to that of EAT, in stressing the vulner-
ability to interference, rather than the likelihood
of interference, by the employer in assessing the
independence of staff associations. These changes
have not, however, gone sufficiently far, in the
view of unions like BIFU, in curtailing the ability
of staff associations to obtain certificates of
independence.

The pressures for amalgamations and transfers
of engagements within the British trade union
movement at the present time are well known, with
certain individual unions seeing this as their
major possible route to any membership growth in
the foreseeable future; recessions (as opposed to
expansionary periods) are typically held to produce
mergers of unions that supplement (as opposed to

complement) each other. In the building societies, unions like BIFU and ASTMS are certainly looking to limit the emergence of any new staff associations and to bring about mergers with existing staff associations. The rules of the latter typically require a ballot of the membership and the support of two-thirds of either those voting or eligible to vote to effect a transfer of engagements. However, as the example of the previous section shows, even a vote in favour of such a transfer will not necessarily result in a procedural agreement coming about if management attitudes remain unshakeably opposed to any form of external representation. In such circumstances situation specific strategies will have to be devised by unions, possibly involving some form of the corporate power strategy (where possible) which we outlined in Chapter 2.

This discussion of the union position in the finance sector was undertaken with two basic purposes in mind. The first was to try and more sharply delineate some of the issues involved in the question of whether individual unions have the capacity to increase union density through their own growth orientated initiatives. The second was to illustrate the importance of an environmental change in enhancing the capability of a management, always motivated to remain non-union, to achieve this end. The particular environmental change focused on was a legal/administrative one concerning the issuance of certificates of independence.

If employers are becoming increasingly doubtful of the value and desirability of trade union recognition, does this mean that an enhanced non-union element in the UK system of industrial relations is inevitable? Or can, and should, trade unions attempt to respond to this possibility by moving away from traditional forms of recognition? This latter question is likely to be to the centre of discussion, debate and controversy in the union movement for a number of years to come. At the present moment this discussion and debate largely revolves around the issue of single recognition agreements, which we consider below.

The Demand and Supply of
Single Recognition Agreements

The alleged costs to management (and the national economy) of multi-unionism have been a much discussed and criticised feature of the traditional system of industrial relations in the UK. The

perceived costs of such a situation are held to
be particularly influential with Japanese companies
contemplating the setting up of a plant in the UK,
given their background of enterprise or company
unionism.   Under the influence of Japanese management practices, among other factors, a belief in
the 'efficiency' (with all the ambiguities associated with this term) of industrial union structures
(a la the West German model) appears to have given
way to one favouring moves in the direction of
trying to establish an individual union-company
identification process.   In the United States, for
example, it has been suggested that:(22)

> bargaining to regain competitiveness will mean
> a change from the present lack of identifi-
> cation with a particular firm to an under-
> standing that employment security and the
> unions governance role are tied directly to
> individual firms.   Unions may at first feel
> they have lost power in representing their
> members.   In the long run, however, they
> will gain broader but more diffuse power to
> influence the most crucial variable of the
> relationship between management and labor;
> the survival of the firm and, consequently,
> the jobs of union members.

In keeping with this sort of view the Shadow
Labour Cabinet has been reported (The Times, 28th
May 1985) as considering a document proposing a
'bill of rights' for employees, the quid pro quo
for which may entail explicit recognition of the
commercial performance of the individual company in
wage demands.   In the short term single recognition
agreements, or at least those of a particular type,
have been viewed as constituting a first step,
albeit a limited one, in the direction of trying
to establish such an identification process.   A
number of recent studies have suggested, rather
than established, the likelihood of single recognition agreements being on the increase in the UK.
The Undy et al study, referred to earlier, specifically cited as an example of 'growth orientated'
union activities the case of a regional secretary
of the GMWU pushing for single recognition agreements with newly relocated plants in the Northern
region.(23)   Moreover, a recent paper by a group
at Durham University reported that the Northern
Economic Development Council listed some 239 single
recognition agreements among companies in that

region;(24)   what proportion this number constituted was not indicated, nor was there any evidence
provided of the changing position (if any) through
time.   And finally, a small survey in the Deeside
area of North Wales found considerable support for
the virtues of single recognition agreements among
the personnel/industrial relations managers
contacted.(25)

A discussion of single recognition agreements
in the UK inevitably leads one to consider the
package deal approach of the EETPU.   The components
of these package agreements are typically single
union recognition, staff status arrangements,
flexible work practices, an advisory board of
elected staff representatives (who are not necessarily union members) to discuss various aspects of
the plant's conditions and performance, and negotiating procedures involving compulsory final offer
(or pendulum) arbitration, the latter allied with
a commitment to avoid industrial action and dis-
ruption; the agreement with Sanyo (Lowestoft) in
1982, for example, states that '... adequate and
speedy procedures for the discussion of company
related affairs and the resolution of problems
precludes the necessity for recourse to any form
of industrial action by either the company, the
union or the employees.'   The latter has inevitably led to them being labelled and criticised as
'no-strike' deals; unions who have had a membership interest in the plants where such deals have
come about have, predictably, been the most vocal
critics of the EETPU.   Much of this criticism is
due to the 'politics' of the EETPU, which has even
taken to attending fringe group meetings at the
annual CBI conference.   A second source of criticism stems from the view that such provisions are
unprecedented divergences from traditional union
practices, and as such, in betraying the fundamental
principles of independent trade unionism, must be
condemned.   A final, and more substantive, worry
and concern is that such agreements may constitute
the 'thin end of the wedge' (whereby there become
virtually no minimal level terms and conditions in
procedural agreements) in an environment of falling
union density, increased spatial dispersion of
membership and increased inter-union competition
for recruitment and recognition; the fear here
is that unions may become involved in a competitive
scramble involving the offer of more and more
favourable terms to management in return for single
recognition being granted.   The EETPU response to

such criticisms, which admittedly has not been particularly well articulated, would presumably take the form that these agreements are not completely unprecedented (recall here the earlier mentioned BIFU [NUBE] procedural agreement with one building society in the early 1970s), that unions must inevitably adapt their practices to a substantially changed environment (in this sense past practices cannot be viewed as 'tablets of stone') and that surely such agreements are worthwhile if the alternative is no recognition; the latter point is pursued here and in the next chapter.

These deals have certainly generated an inordinate amount of criticism relative to their number. An article published in May 1985 indicated that the EETPU had signed 11 such agreements,(26) although press reports some 2 months later quoted the general secretary as saying that there were 14 in existence, another 4 in the pipeline and at least half a dozen more which they were hoping to complete. The 14 agreements in existence are estimated to cover some 10,000 employees, mainly in electronics and high technology companies. The EETPU have conceded that there are limitations to their approach, most notably the fact that the agreements are only regarded as a feasible option by management in newly established plants.

The most detailed study of the employment practices of newly established plants is that by Morgan and Sayer who have examined the electrical engineering industry in South Wales.(27) Their findings for the more recent entrants to this industry indicate the particular importance attached to detailed and careful recruitment procedures, the priority attached to achieving flexible working practices, the existence of simplified pay structures, the emphasis on direct communications with the workforce, and the incidence of single recognition agreements. In the latter case they found a strong management preference for dealing with the EETPU, which was typically attributed to '... its positive attitude to profits and flexibility, its use of its own resources to train and retrain for multi-skilled grades and, because EETPU officials are appointed rather than elected, they could afford to take a firmer line with their members, thereby delivering a more disciplined workforce'.(28) Their work does, however, suggest the existence of some role conflict problems for EETPU shop stewards who are not as actively and positively committed

as the full-time union officers to the various
components of these package deals.

Morgan and Sayer go on to contrast the extent
of the union presence (albeit in this new form) in
the South Wales electronic industry with that in
electronic industry plants in Scotland and Berkshire
the latter being referred to as the 'English
sunbelt'.   Although no detailed analysis is
attempted, the lesser union presence in Scotland
is attributed to (i) the relatively high proportion
of US owned plants there (some figures provided by
the Locate in Scotland Bureau suggest that some 40%
of the electronics industry in Scotland is US owned)
and (ii) the social composition of the workforce
in the new towns of Scotland.   The conspicuous
absence of trade unions among the electronics firms
in Berkshire is attributed to the relative absence
of an employee demand for union recognition which
stems, in turn, from the relatively high proportion
of professional workers, the lack of a union
tradition in the area, and the high proportion of
small sized firms.   The importance of these factors
in contributing to non-union status will be examined
at some length in the next chapter.

Conclusions
In our scene setting chapter we stressed that
consideration of any management initiated changes
away from a union acceptance ideology at the
organisational level must involve an examination
of the incentives, enabling conditions and particular manifestations of such a change.   This
chapter, and the previous one, have largely sought
to document one particular manifestation of such
a change, namely the existence of considerable (one
cannot strictly speaking say increased, due to the
absence of adequate time series data) management
opposition to union attempts to achieve recognition
in previously uncovered bargaining units.

The strongest evidence in support of this
conclusion came from examining the public policy
based route to recognition, although this has its
potential limitations as a basis for generalisation:
recall the relatively small numbers involved, and
the fact that, as 'weapon of last resort', it may
involve a disproportionate number of employers most
strongly opposed to unions.   For this reason, as
well as the desire to look at some related matters
(e.g. possible factors assisting such a move, and
the response of individual unions) we undertook a
more qualitative discussion of the finance sector

and made a preliminary incursion into the subject
area of new plants. The latter is potentially
important, at least on US evidence, as being to the
forefront of management opposition to the institution of unionism.

In fact the evidence we have reviewed here,
and in the previous chapter, on management opposition to union attempts to achieve recognition in
previously unorganised units mixes partially
unionised and non-union establishments, single
independent establishments and multi-plant companies
and has made only passing reference to a possible
ownership influence on the management desire to
avoid recognition. In an attempt to be more
precise about such possible influences on management's position with regard to unions the next
chapter specifically deals with the subject of
non-union establishments. In this treatment we
are centrally concerned with the question of whether
the non-union component of the UK system of
industrial relations is on the increase.

NOTES

1.   J.F.B. Goodman and J. Krislov, "Conciliation in Industrial Disputes in Great Britain: A
Survey of the Attitudes of the Parties", British
Journal of Industrial Relations, Vol.XII, No.3,
November 1974, p.335.
2.   Goodman and Krislov, op.cit., p.342.
3.   Quoted in G.S. Bain, "Trade Union Growth
and Recognition", Research Paper No. 6, Royal
Commission on Trade Unions and Employers Associations, HMSO, London, 1967, p.100·
4.   See, for example, Thomas A. Kochan and
Todd Jick, "The Public Sector Mediation Process:
A Theory and Empirical Examination", Journal of
Conflict Resolution, Vol.22, June 1978, pp.209-240.
5.   Bain, Loc.cit.
6.   ACAS Annual Report 1980, HMSO, London,
1981, p.65.
7.   ACAS Annual Report 1983, HMSO, London,
1984, p.28.
8.   W.W. Daniel and Neil Millward, Workplace
Industrial Relations in Britain, Heinemann, London,
1983, p.32.
9.   Clive Jenkins and Barrie Sherman, White
Collar Unionism, Routledge and Kegan Paul, London,
1979, p.53.

10.   G.S. Bain, The Growth of White Collar Unionism, Oxford University Press, Oxford, 1970.

11.   R. Undy et al, Change in Trade Unions, Hutchinson, London, 1981, pp.161-162.

12.   See W. Graham Astley and Andrew H. Van de Ven, "Central Perspectives and Debates in Organisation Theory", Administrative Science Quarterly, Vol.28, June 1983, pp.245-273.

13.   Robert Taylor, The Fifth Estate, Pan, London, 1980, p.384.

14.   Robert T. Buchanan, "Mergers in British Trade Unions, 1949-1979", Industrial Relations Journal, Vol.12, No.3, May/June 1981, p.46.

15.   Margaret A. Ford, "Recruiting in Recession: Some Trade Union Experience from the Finance Sector", Unpublished M.Phil in Industrial Relations Dissertation, University of Glasgow, 1984.

16.   The Times, 5th July 1985.

17.   See, for example, CIR Report No.86, p.12.

18.   Industrial Relations Review and Report, No.63, September 1973.

19.   A.I.R. Swabe and Patricia Price, "Building a Permanent Association? The Development of Staff Associations in the Building Societies", British Journal of Industrial Relations, Vol.22, No.2, July 1984, p.195.

20.   Annual Report of the Trades Union Congress, 1976, p.454.

21.   Staff Associations, Supplement to the Annual Report of the Certification Officer, 1979, p.40.

22.   D. Quinn Mills and Malcolm Lovell, "Enhancing Competitiveness: The Contribution of Employee Relations", in Bruce R. Scott and George C. Lodge (eds), US Competitiveness in the World Economy, Harvard Business School Press, Boston, 1984, p.464.

23.   Undy et al, op.cit., p.136.

24.   David Bright, Derek Sawbridge and Bill Rees, "Industrial Relations of Recession", Industrial Relations Journal, Vol.14, No.3, Autumn 1983, p.27.

25.   Ed Rose and Chris Selby, "Some Reflections Upon Trade Union Recognition", Industrial Relations Journal, Vol.16, No.1, Spring 1985.

26.   Robert Taylor, "The Union No-Strike Force", Management Today, April 1985, p.84.

27.   Kevin Morgan and Andrew Sayer, "A Modern Industry in a Mature Region", Urban and Regional Studies Working Paper No.39, University of Sussex, 1984.

28.   Morgan and Sayer, op.cit., p.21.

Chapter Five

NON-UNION FIRMS IN THE UK

As noted in Chapter 1, the employee relations of
non-union firms, indeed almost the very existence
of such firms, has been largely ignored by industrial relations scholars in the UK.   The reasons
for this neglect would appear to include the fact
that the high water mark of industrial relations
research in the UK (1965-1979) was in years of
growing union membership (and associated structures
and behaviour), with the union (albeit very largely
the lay representatives) being overwhelmingly seen
as the leading agent of change in the system.   The
predictable consequence was a relative under-
researching of the management function, particularly
where no collective bargaining relationship was
involved.   A second possible reason for the neglect
of non-union firms has been the very limited
presence of behavioural scientists in the industrial
relations research community of the UK.   It is
these sorts of individuals, with their organisation
behaviour orientation and training, who are the
obvious people to be most interested and capable of
conducting research on aspects of employee relations
in non-union plants.   In fact they have very much
kept their distance from the industrial relations
field in the UK which they believe in practice has
come to be virtually equated, as a result of the
dominant position of the institutionalists, with
collective bargaining research.
     The results of the DE/PSI/SSRC workplace
industrial relations survey of 1980 has provided
the opportunity to begin work in this area.   In
Chapter 1 we noted the work of Deaton on management
styles, which utilised this particular source of
information.   Further work by Deaton involving an
examination of the determinants of manual recognition (the inverse being a reasonable proxy for

non-union status) in the manufacturing and private
services sectors found that non-union status was
positively associated with small establishment size
(in both sectors), foreign ownership (manufacturing
only) and more recently established plants (manufacturing only).(1)   These three relationships, as
well as the earlier discussed work of Morgan and
Sayer, helped inform much of the work undertaken in
this chapter.   It is also worth noting that some
basic results from the 1980 survey suggested that
the most favourable assessments, by management, of
both industrial relations and financial performance
were associated with non-union establishments.(2)

Adding to the Stock of Non-Union Firms

According to Deaton's figures from the 1980 workplace industrial relations survey some 29% of establishments were non-union ones.   What is the likelihood that this figure will have increased if a
similarly based survey is undertaken in, for example
1990?   An answer to this question requires considering the three potential sources of addition to
the population of establishments in the UK: (i)
British multi-plant companies;   (ii) British single,
independent establishments;   and (iii) multi-
national corporations.

    In the case of multi-establishment organi-
sations growth can occur through acquisitions or
the building of new plants.   The years 1965-1975
saw a good deal of urban and regional research in
the UK concentrating on the phenomena of multi-
establishment organisations building new (branch)
plants.   This concentration on the building of
new plants is maintained by the 'greenfield site'
literature in the UK where it is contended that
such sites involve an attempt to establish a 'wider
framework of employer-employee relations' stemming
from the experience of problems and difficulties
in older, more conventionally designed and run
establishments.   The negative elements from which
escape is being sought through greenfield site
establishments appear to be factors such as deteri-
orating payment systems, restrictive practices,
strong and well established shop steward organisations, multi-unionism, overmanning and low
productivity.   The 'philosophy' associated with
individual greenfield sites and other new plants
has certainly received a good deal of attention.
An illustration of such a philosophy is that of
the new float glass plant of Pilkingtons, whose

physical location probably means it is not a greenfield site in the strictest sense of the term,
which was as follows:(3)

(i)   increased 'site commitment';
(ii)   better co-operation between trade unions;
(iii)   well trained employees who fully understand
         their role in the works as a whole;
(iv)   flexible employees - able to do a wide range
         of tasks;
(v)   management style based on openness and
         employee involvement;
(vi)   push responsibility down the hierarchy;
(vii)   remove status differences which cannot be
         justified;
(viii)   simple, effective, easily understood reward
         system;
(ix)   eliminate payment for overtime.

     The existing greenfield site (and new plant)
literature is overwhelmingly based on a small
number of highly descriptive case studies (as above)
and as such, does not systematically address the
following questions: What is the numerical significance of this phenomenon? And what is the
potential for operating such establishments (in
contrast to the position in existing plants) on a
non-union basis? The urban and regional literature
tends to suggest that the building of new plants
by multi-plant organisations has become of much
less numerical importance from the mid-1970s,
particularly so since the onset of the current
recession. In Storey's study of newcomers to
Cleveland county in the period 1972-1979, for
example, the number of single, independent establishments exceeded the number of branch plant establishments.(4) The numerical importance of the
former group goes a considerable way to explaining
why urban and regional scholars have increasingly
turned their attention to single, independent
establishments as the important factor in the
differing capacity of areas to stimulate employment
growth. This urban and regional research is also
important in providing some much needed perspective
on the notion of 'high technology' industries and
plants. In fact the definition of a 'high technology establishment' is a far from straightforward
exercise. However, one recent study of the East
Anglia area (where such plants are alleged to be
disproportionately concentrated), using a minimum
list heading classification basis, estimated that

only some 10% of the newly established (and surviv-
ing) firms in that area in the period 1971-1981
appeared to come into this category.(5)   The
contents of Table 5.1 provide some useful information on the high technology establishments that are
located in the Cambridge area.

Table 5.1:   Cambridge High-Tech Companies,
              by Sector and Age, 1984

	% of companies	% of employment	% of turnover
Chemicals/biotech	4	9	15
Electricals	3	2	2
Electronics/ capital goods	22	21	14
Other electronics	10	11	16
Instrument engineering	17	22	14
Computer hardware	11	7	23
Software	23	8	8
Consultancy/R & D	6	17	7
Other	4	3	1
	100	100	100
Totals	261	13,700	£890m

By age, 1984	Number	Employment	Turnover (£m)
All companies	261	13,700	890
Established 1974-1978	61	2,750	242
Established since 1979	128	2,030	102

Source: Your Business, September 1985, p.32.

_____

     Unfortunately, no information was provided on
their union status, although, in addition to the
above information, it is worth noting that more
than three-quarters are single, independent establishments.   As we have seen in the United States,
management has the ability to close a unionised
establishment in, for example, Pittsburgh and open
up a new one on a non-union basis in a place like
Houston.   In the UK this would appear to be a much
more difficult exercise for management to undertake;
the anecdotal story related by Handy in the Gods
of Management (p.102) is an excellent illustration
of this differing capacity.   This is because,

firstly, the smaller geographical size of the UK
economy (together with the absence of state level
'right to work' legislation) means that 'recognition by extension' (from one plant to another) is
likely to be a more common phenomenon than in the
United States; the 1980 workplace industrial
relations survey indicates recognition by extension
for manuals in some 18% of establishments, and in
some 11% of establishments for non-manuals.(6)
Indeed, as Tony Lane has argued:(7)

> The move into the country has not necessarily
> meant the establishment of non-union plants.
> While it would be reasonable to expect lower
> levels of unionisation in these areas, in-
> going plants, especially those of larger
> companies with established recognition agree-
> ments and elaborate industrial relations
> systems, will often have stitched up recog-
> nition deals for outlying plants before they
> have even opened their gates. A captive
> membership may gladden the heart of union
> finance officers ... but it will do little for
> those long-sighted enough to appreciate the
> value of spontaneity.

This perspective does question the character
(or, in Blackburn's terms, the unionateness) of
organisation that results from such recognition by
extension, but certainly suggests that some form
of recognition is likely to result from this
process; admittedly the acquisition (as opposed
to building) of some branch establishments, particularly of small size, may not necessarily be caught
up in such a process.

And secondly, as we mentioned in previous
chapters, the existence of national level redundancy
legislation, including an obligation on employers
to consult with recognised unions over the means
of implementing such redundancies, would appear to
limit, relative to the United States, the capacity
for management to 'close union and open non-union'
in the UK.   This legislation, as well as the actual
occurrence of redundancies, appears to have stimulated the development of formal, joint redundancy
agreements in the UK which typically contain
provisions banning the recruitment of new labour,
and giving priority to the redeployment of redundant
workers into any available vacancies.   The movement towards single employer bargaining structures
in the 1970s certainly appears to have been associated with an increased scope of bargaining, partic-

ularly over levels of output and manning.(8)   The
1980 workplace industrial relations survey indicates the very considerable extent of bargaining
over redundancy matters,(9) whereas in the United
States advance notice and union participation
provisions relating to closing or relocation
decisions are found in fewer than 8% of major
collective agreements;(10)   the latter figure
clearly helps to explain the current union interest
in the United States in plant closing legislation.
   For these reasons we do not envisage that
British, multi-establishment corporations with a
substantial, existing union presence have any
significant capacity to add to the stock of non-
union establishments in the UK.   There is, however,
one qualifying comment that we would attach to this
general conclusion, this being that 'recognition
by extension' in the UK is likely to be more of a
manual phenomenon of the past, rather than a non-
manual phenomenon of the future.   The reasons for
this are management's considerable resistance to
union recognition for an individual group of non-
manual employees, on the grounds that such employees
are a company or group-wide resource and hence a
meaningful or viable bargaining unit can only exist
at such a level;   the importance of this fact is
enhanced by the relative growth of white collar
employment in the economy as a whole.
   The view adopted here is that any additions to
the stock of non-union establishments in the UK is
mostly likely to come from single, independent
establishments and foreign incomers to the UK.
These are the two groups that are, therefore, discussed at some length in this chapter.   However,
before turning to them we consider the group of
well-known, non-union firms in the UK that are
alleged to be the current 'pace setters' in terms
of employee relations.

The Household Name Group
The firms that we have in mind here obviously
include IBM, Marks and Spencer, Gillette and Hewlett
Packard.   Although subject to little detailed
academic scrutiny their employment policies are
reasonably well known as a result of accounts by
journalists (11) and the numerous (and increasing)
presentations in recent years by members of these
particular companies to a variety of seminar and
conference audiences.   It is often thought or
implied that these firms have simply 'bought off'
unionism by paying relatively high wages.   These

117

firms certainly make considerable use of wage
surveys of comparable (along industry, occupation
and area dimensions) employers, with the resulting
wages often being set within the top quartile of
the surveyed group.   This is most certainly the
case at IBM, where wages are estimated to be at
least some 10% above those paid by the comparable
employers they have surveyed.   Marks and Spencer
pay considerably more than the relevant wages council recommendation, although their wages are generally lower than those of Mothercare and C & A.
The favourable fringe benefit provisions of these
particular companies are strongly emphasised by
their management as a factor in 'good employee
relations'.   At Marks and Spencer, for instance,
welfare expenditure is estimated to average around
£1,000 per employee, with individual benefits
including a non-contributory pension scheme, medical
benefits (chiropody, physiotherapy, dentistry and
cervical screening) staff hairdressing facilities,
subsidised lunches, sickness and death benefits.
In the case of Hewlett Packard fringe benefits are
estimated to add around 50% more to straight wage
payments.

These particular companies place great stress
on trying to achieve 'good communications' between
management and the workforce; one IBM manager I
have spoken to was of the view that the vast
majority (i.e. more than 75%) of all industrial
disputes in British industry are the result of a
communications failure.   This orientation is
frequently reflected in a low manager/employee
ratio (1:10 at Hewlett Packard's South Queensferry
plant, for example) and/or a high ratio of personnel
staff to employees (1:60 in the case of Marks and
Spencer).   In addition, at Gillette, there are
long standing grievance procedures and joint consultative arrangements with employee representatives at the Isleworth and Reading plants.   These
committees meet on a monthly basis to discuss
various matters with management, and once a year
the Managing Director presents a confidential
report on current financial results and future
company prospects to these committees.   At Marks
and Spencer, monthly communication group meetings
are held in each of the company's stores, supplemented with visits by divisional management teams
and by a director.   The most commonly used grievance arrangement at IBM is 'speak up' where
employees can place complaints or suggestions in a
box situated near each notice board.   These

complaints or suggestions are transferred to a
central co-ordinator who then passes the matter to
the relevant manager who must reply to the employee,
via the co-ordinator, within a week.   In 1979, for
example, there were 1,119 'speak ups', of which 266
were complaints, 347 inquiries and 366 comments.
Management took action in 24 per cent of these,
with the major sources of complaint being cafe-
terias, the working environment and office/adminis-
tration procedure (N = 136);   only 25 complaints
concerned pay and benefits, and some 30 were to do
with employee-management relations and communications.   Other individual personnel policies that
appear to be associated with this group of non-
union firms include profit-sharing and stock option
schemes, single (staff) status working arrangements
and a strong commitment to employee job security.
In the latter case both Hewlett Packard and IBM are
well known for their commitments to a no-redundancy
policy;   in September 1985 management of the former
announced that in order to avoid lay-offs the South
Queensferry plant (and others in the UK) will close
for 1 day a month, the equivalent of a 5% wage cut
for the employees.   IBM, Hewlett-Packard and
Gillette also make periodic use of employee opinion
surveys or ballots to monitor the state of employee
satisfaction with various aspects of their job.

The arrangements and policies highlighted
above seem to fit well with discussions of the
characteristics necessary to produce strong organisational identification and commitment on the part
of employees.   There are typically held to be four
major elements in achieving individual employee
identification with the particular company of
employment: (12)

(i)   selecting individuals who, ideologically,
         'match' the organisation's goals and values
         and/or who can be trained in and indoctrin-
         ated with the corporate philosophy;
(ii)   providing individuals with the opportunity
         to work for a high status organisation,
         and providing new members with high status
         opportunities within that system;
(iii)   providing challenging, involving work that
         continually stimulates the individual;
(iv)   providing an extremely pleasant work environ-
         ment and formal reward system that satisfies
         all individual 'comfort' needs, both on and
         off the job.

The emphasis placed on trying to achieve such identification is why, as we saw in Chapter 2, a number of these companies (e.g. IBM, and Hewlett Packard) figure so prominently in Ouchi's discussion of Theory Z principles. The organisational characteristics of Theory Z companies (which we listed in Chapter 2) are viewed by Ouchi as essentially deriving from the enunciation and implementation of a particular corporate philosophy by senior management. The Hewlett Packard philosophy is approvingly cited by Ouchi, where the objective for employees is 'to help HP people share in the company's success, which they make possible; to provide job security based on their performance; to recognise their individual achievements; and to insure the personal satisfaction that comes from a sense of accomplishment in their work.'

As to their attitudes towards unions, the following summary statement of the IBM position is worthy of particular note: (13)

> there was an implicit assumption in the concept of unionisation that the interests of the employed would inevitably be neglected by the employer in the absence of trade union representation. IBM rejected the argument that this assumption had a universal validity. It considered that IBM had demonstrated that a company could be managed successfully in the best interests of employees without trade union representation. To substantiate this statement, the company pointed to what it considered to be an excellent record of harmonious strike-free employee relations, in particular the maintenance of full employment through a policy of flexibility in the deployment of labour, and an exceptionally low labour turnover. In the IBM personnel philosophy, the company states, emphasis was placed on the individual, on the rewarding of individual effort, and on close employee-management relations characterised by mutual trust. The company expressed the fear that unionisation would create a hitherto non-existent diversiveness between employees and management by shifting emphasis on to groups. It was the company's view that the unity and flexibility of its single status workforce was of paramount value.

Non-Union Firms in the UK

The desire here is to avoid unions as an external constraint perceived as likely to limit the response time of an organisation requiring above all else flexibility because of its operation in an environment of rapidly changing technology and product market conditions (e.g. relatively short product life cycles). The above statement was in fact given to ACAS in 1977 in the course of a statutory recognition claim investigation, an investigation which produced the following employee ballot results:

		Greenock	Rest of Company
1.	Response rate	98.4%	94.6%
2.	Currently a trade union member	2.5%	0.5%
3.	Wishing collective bargaining coverage	8.9%	3.5%
4.	Willing to join a union if it was recognised by the company	8.1%	4.4%

In noting such a strong 'no-vote' for trade union recognition, it is worth recalling that the company was estimated to have spent some £10,000 on an information-publicity campaign to this end. This fact notwithstanding, additional questions in the ballot clearly revealed extremely low levels of criticism of the company's personnel and pay policies. In other words, the nature of the voice (and other) mechanisms provided at IBM (as alternatives to quitting or trade union representation) were clearly adequate, at least at this point in time, to the task of preventing the emergence of a level of job dissatisfaction likely to lead, in turn, to a demand for union recognition. One needs to emphasise here the phrase 'at this point in time' because one cannot necessarily assume that such a level of demand will remain constant through time. The case of Kodak Limited, which is the largest subsidiary of Eastman Kodak outside the United States, must give some heart to trade union officers, lest they come to believe that these particular companies are inherently incapable of being unionised.

Kodak Limited was established in Britain at the turn of the century, with unions not being recognised there prior to 1972. Prior to that date Kodak had a system of workers' representation committees, whose origins were in wartime production committees. There were in fact 11 such committees (over the 5 different locations of the company), consisting entirely of employees and operating with a written constitution (from 1951) that provided for discussion '... on working conditions and general wage level changes instigated by management.' It was in fact legislation, namely the Industrial Relations Act 1971 and the Trade Union and Labor Relations Act 1974, that stimulated the two major changes there; the transformation of the workers representation committees into the Union of Kodak Workers (1972) and the merger with the TGWU in August 1974. The Kodak case also suggests the potential importance of organisation specific sources of job dissatisfaction in stimulating a demand for unionisation. In this particular case apparently considerable employee dissatisfaction built up over the inability of the workers' representation committees to obtain compensation for industrial accidents; in 1970, for instance, there were 321 reportable industrial accidents in Kodak, but less than 10% of these had involved compensation claims.(14) The relatively small number of claims put forward, much less won by employees, clearly stimulated an employee interest in obtaining access to the legal services of trade unions.

In addition to trade unions needing to be alert to such company specific sources of dissatisfaction there is also the importance of the appropriate timing of any recognition initiative taken in relation to such companies. J.C. Bamford Excavators was a non-union establishment for more than 30 years, which in the early '70s responded to an increasing demand for unionisation by providing all production workers with staff status, longer paid holidays, sickness pay, life insurance coverage and improved pension arrangements. However in 1974 the company's employee works committee sought a pay increase beyond the Government pay limits at the time. This was rejected by management, a decision that led to the GMWU obtaining a single union recognition agreement there.

For a long time, the trade union movement in the UK could comfort themselves in the knowledge that the firms we have been discussing here were a relatively small, self-contained group that had few imitators in the rest of the system. Throughout the 1960s and 1970s the pacesetters in industrial relations who seemed worthy and likely of imitation by the rest of the management community were unionised companies; one thinks here of productivity bargaining at Esso, Fawley, or organisation development and change initiatives in Shell. However, as indicated in our introduction, there is now a belief, not to say fear, among unions that other companies are beginning to look more to the IBMs as the example to follow in employment matters. In Chapter 4, for example, we noted Morgan and Sayers' comment regarding the presence of non-union, US owned establishments in the electronics industry in Scotland, particularly in the new town locations. The obvious questions raised by that comment concern the numerical extent of such a presence and, secondly, are they following the union substitution approach of companies like IBM? The next section attempts to provide some answers to these questions.

The US Incomers

At the present time it is estimated that around 16% of manufacturing employment in the UK is accounted for by foreign owned establishments. Scotland has a relatively long history of foreign owned employment establishments, with the number of such establishments exceeding those in other major Assisted Areas of the UK. In 1981 there were some 288 foreign owned establishments in the manufacturing sector in Scotland.(15) The average size of these foreign owned establishments was 326, compared to 103 for UK owned establishments; this significant size difference meant that foreign owned establishments accounted for some 17% of manufacturing employment in Scotland, but only 7% of the total number of employment units. The date of opening of these foreign owned establishments is set out below in Table 5.2.

The largest single group in the Table opened up prior to 1950, although important additions to the stock occurred in the years 1965-1979. This pattern of plant opening dates suggests that any significant non-union, US presence in Scotland may in fact predate the current recession. As regards US owned establishments, 170 of the 288 foreign owned establishments in 1981 (i.e. 59%) came from this particular source, accounting for some 73% of the total employment associated with foreign owned establishments in the manufacturing sector in Scotland.

The results of a number of general surveys of industrial relations phenomena in Britain (such as

123

Table 5.2:   Overseas-owned Units in Operation
              in Scotland, by Year of Opening,
              (to 1981)

Period of Opening	Number of Units	% of total
Pre - 1950	80	27
1950 - 1954	8	3
1955 - 1959	22	8
1960 - 1964	21	7
1965 - 1969	46	16
1970 - 1974	61	21
1975 - 1979	42	15
1980 or later	8	3

Source: Neil Hood and Stephen Young, Multinationals
          in Retreat: The Scottish Experience,
          Edinburgh University Press, Edinburgh,
          1982, p.10.

---

that conducted at Warwick University in 1977/1978)
have indicated that foreign owned plants have been
relatively progressive or innovative in the sense of
being, for example, to the forefront in the development of single employer bargaining structures, and
in having a relatively well developed personnel
management function.   In addition to these findings, there have been a number of industrial relations studies specifically concerned with foreign
owned plants in Britain.   These specialist studies
have been overwhelmingly concerned with two basic
questions: (i) the strike frequency of foreign
owned plants compared to their British counterparts;
and (ii) the degree of centralisation/decentralis-
ation in industrial relations decision making within
these particular organisations.   There are various
criticisms that have been made of these specialist
studies, most notably their narrow focus and essentially atheoretical approach.   To these can be
added the fact that they have overwhelmingly concentrated on unionised establishments.
      On the question of non-union status, there are
some existing survey results for Scotland that can
be usefully mentioned.   The first is a survey by
the Scottish Development Agency in 1983 of 133 US
manufacturing plants in Scotland.(16)   The basic
finding was that some 44% of these were non-union,
with this figure rising to 63% in electronics
plants, 73% in oil related plants and 86% in health

care plants. A second survey was conducted in the early 1980s in East Kilbride New Town (recall here the comment of Morgan and Sayers on Scottish New Towns) and found that 69% of the 93 manufacturing plants examined were non-union.(17) These non-union plants were far from being simply small sized ones; the proportion of non-union plants was particularly high in instrument engineering, electrical engineering and the electronics industry. Two of the leading non-union plants highlighted in this survey were the US owned ones, Gray Tool (247 employees) and Motorola (1,269 employees). The former paid wages some 10% above the industry average (and with fringe benefits accounting for some 15-20% of employment costs), while the latter paid 15-20% above the industry average (fringe benefits accounted for some 30% of employment costs); both reported low levels of absenteeism (1% and 5% respectively) and labour turnover (0.5% and 2% respectively). Neither of these surveys specifically examined the date of opening of these non-union establishments in Scotland. However, such information was provided by the Scottish Development Agency for the 33 US electronics firms in Scotland (in 1983) which each had more than 50 employees; this set of information distinguished between those firms established pre- and post-1970. More than half of these were non-union (N = 18), with the correlation coefficient between such status and post-1970 establishment being positively signed, but insignificant (r = 0.258). The implication from this data source is that the US non-union presence in Scotland certainly pre-dates the current recession, although this is clearly the period of time in which it has been most discussed in the media. One should not, however, exaggerate the extent to which the New Towns in Scotland are characterised by a US electronic industry (or high technology) presence. A recent examination, utilising information largely provided by trade union officers, was made of the 2 New Towns of Irvine and Glenrothes.(18) This study revealed, firstly, that a substantial number of all the existing plants in these towns had been established since 1979; 49% in Irvine and 54% in the case of Glenrothes. And secondly, a relatively high proportion of the plants opened since 1979 were non-union establishments; the relevant figures here being 84% and 82% respectively. These non-union establishments were predominantly British owned, single independent establishments covering

a sizeable range of manufacturing and service
industries.   There was in fact only one foreign
owned establishment set up in Glenrothes after 1979,
and only 9 such establishments in Irvine.   These
new, small firms will be discussed at some length
later in this chapter.

In order to try and obtain an indication of
the employment practices associated with US non-
union firms in Scotland a small survey was undertaken with the co-operation of the Scottish Development Agency.   A postal questionnaire covering a
variety of employment practices was sent to some
87 firms with which the Agency had dealings.   A
response rate of 72% was obtained (N = 63), with
the leading characteristics of the respondents being
those set out below in Table 5.3.

Table 5.3:   Basic Characteristics of Respondents
             to the SDA Survey

% manufacturing sector	92
% US owned	32
% non-union	57
% single plant (in UK)	67
% established post-1976	44
Mean (median) size	257 (100)

Source: P.B. Beaumont and B. Townley, 'Greenfield
          Sites, New Plants and Work Practices',
          in V. Hammond (ed), Current Research in
          Management, Pinter, London.

The questionnaire enquired about the existence
(or not) of 12 listed employment practices (see
Table 5.4) and the largest single group of respondents (21%) indicated that they had 5 of these.
An examination of the characteristics of plants with
a relatively large number of these practices (i.e.
5 or more) revealed that they were US owned
($r = 0.263$) and non-union ($r = 0.234$);   these two
characteristics were themselves significantly
correlated ($r = 0.239$).   Furthermore, non-union
status was significantly and positively associated
with the individual practices of staff status
($r = 0.398$), and autonomous work groups ($r = 0.353$),
while US ownership was related to the existence of
quality circles ($r = 0.541$).

There were in fact some 36 non-union plants
in the survey and when we examined them in some
detail we found that they fell into two basic
groups, differentiated by size and ownership.

The first consisted of 15 US owned establishments, with an average size of 414 employees, while the second comprised 17 British owned establishments with an average size of 59 employees.   The very considerable size difference between the two groups of non-union establishments raises the strong possibility that their work practices, and hence underlying human resource management strategy, will be very different.   An investigation of this possibility revealed, firstly, that the average number of work practices in our US non-union establishments in Scotland (N = 5.5) exceeded the average number for the British owned non-union establishments (N = 3.5).   And, secondly, fully 67% of the US non-union establishments had 5 or more of the listed work practices, whereas the comparable figure for the British owned ones was only 41%.   As regards the individual work practices the results obtained are those set out in Table 5.4.
    There are a number of observations that can be made about the above figures.   The first is that the US non-union establishments have in all cases but one (i.e. staff status arrangements) more of the listed work practices than the British non-union establishments;   the differences, however, are relatively little in the case of some of the work practices (e.g. an added value scheme) given the small base numbers involved.   Secondly, the most common work practices differ between the two groups of non-union establishments.   For the British non-union firms the most common practices are employee briefing groups, staff status arrange-ments, a training scheme and a consultative committ-ee.   In the case of the US non-union establishments the most common practices are a joint health and safety committee, a training scheme, employee briefing groups and problem solving groups.   And finally, when a comparison is made with the figures for the sample as a whole, the US non-union figures are always above the sample average, whereas in a number of cases the British non-union firms fall below it.
    These findings suggest that there is relatively little overlap between the number and nature of employment practices associated with US owned non-union and British owned non-union firms in the UK. In the next section of this chapter we present some further evidence that appears to reinforce this particular conclusion.   However, in the remainder of this section we seek to offer an explanation of this limited overlap phenomenon.

Table 5.4:   Individual Work Practices and
             Non-Union Establishments

Work Practice	(1) British Non-Union	(2) US Non-Union	(3) Sample as a whole
1. Employee briefing groups	71%	73%	71%
2. A joint consultative committee	41%	47%	41%
3. A joint health and safety committee	18%	93%	67%
4. A job evaluation scheme	24%	40%	32%
5. Problem solving groups (e.g.quality circles)	12%	67%	30%
6. A joint productivity committee	12%	13%	13%
7. An in-plant training scheme	47%	80%	60%
8. A profit sharing scheme	24%	27%	17%
9. An added value scheme	6%	7%	6%
10. A share option scheme	12%	20%	9%
11. A common staff status arrangement	59%	53%	43%
12. Autonomous work groups	18%	27%	13%

Source: Beaumont and Townley, Loc.cit.

In attempting to offer an explanation of the
human resource management approach of the US non-
union establishments that we have been considering
above, our hope is to move beyond the rather glib
tendency to simply label them as 'paternalists'.
There are a number of criticisms that can be made
of the use of this particular term, among which we
would particularly highlight its implicit assump-
tion or implication that the driving force (or
priority reason) for having these policies is a
union avoidance motive.   The contention here is
that the nature of working arrangements and practices in such firms stem from more fundamental
considerations, although union avoidance is nevertheless an expected, and desired, outcome.(19)

This particular contention leads us to suggest
the potential value of using Burns and Stalkers
concept of an organic (as opposed to mechanistic)
management system as a reference point for

understanding the incentives for adopting such working practices and arrangements.(20)   The essential difference between the organic and mechanistic management systems, at least for the individual employee, is held to be the greater commitment to the organisation of the former, with the major incentive for the adoption of such a system being the fact that the organisation faces an environment of rapid technical and product market change.   In other words, the flexible working arrangements of such firms (e.g. few and broad job classifications, flexibility in job assignments, etc.) are designed to achieve maximum organisational adaptability in a rapidly changing environment, with the favourable employment rewards package being the quid pro quo for such flexibility and the means (in addition to the nature of the work practices themselves) of ensuring an individual-company identification process.   And if such an identification process does occur across the workforce at large the predictable (and desired) outcome is a relatively limited demand for union services due to the essential absence of job dissatisfaction.

Burns and Stalker view the senior management of the company as being the vital change agent or means of bringing about the existence of an organic management system.   The senior management role in this regard is a function of their perceptions of the environment as well as certain of their values and beliefs with regard to individual employees. In the non-union, US firms of the type being discussed, the senior management belief of particular relevance here is likely to be that unionisation simply results from the failure of management to meet their employees' working needs.   It has, of course, been argued that senior management beliefs and values can be of substantial importance in shaping the particular mix of personnel policies in any employment establishment at a particular point in time.(21)   However, if organisational flexibility and individual employee-company identification (and hence no demand for unionisation) is to be maintained through time these senior management values and beliefs need to be effectively institutionalised (as opposed to personalised) in the organisation.   The major means to this end are likely to be a relatively sizeable, authoritative personnel function and/or a strong emphasis in management evaluation and promotion decisions on the ability to handle employees well.   The capacity

129

to both adopt and maintain an organic management
system requires an adequate degree of organisational
resources, which has been argued to be a function
of organisation size, the capital intensity of
production and the degree of organisation slack.(22)
The degree of organisation slack (resulting from
factors such as competitive advantage) is likely
to be particularly important here as it provides
the area of discretion or room for manoeuvre which
allows the mix of personnel policies to be so much
influenced by the nature of senior management
values.   Certainly casual empiricism in the United
States suggests that the better standards non-union
firms invariably tend to be characterised by rapid
growth and high profits.   On this latter point a
recent paper provided two detailed case studies of
non-union, US firms in Scotland, one of which had
suffered a severe reduction in organisation slack
leading to redundancies and the introduction of pay
and benefit reduction.(23)   However, these adverse
economic circumstances had not produced a demand for
unionisation (the workforce had voted against union
recognition by a factor of some 3 to 1), which
suggests that the organisation culture in favour
of non-union status is much more institutionalised
than is suggested by the view that 'paternalists'
simply 'buy-off' the demand for unionisation.
    What does the above analysis imply for the US
and British owned non-union establishments that
were identified in our Scottish survey?   The
lesser number of work practices associated with the
British owned ones, as well as the differing nature
of their arrangements, would suggest that these
smaller, single independent establishments have less
capacity, and arguably less incentive (due to their
size) to operate as better standards employers,
at least in the formal sense of the term.   The
likelihood of relatively less organisation slack
at any point in time is obviously of potential
importance here.   However, the major question
which needs to be addressed is whether their relatively limited overlap with the work practices of
the US non-union establishments automatically
implies that they should be consigned to the
category of low standards employers, pursuing a
union suppression, as opposed to union substitution,
approach.   Some evidence which bears on this
question is presented in the next section.

New, Small Firms in the UK

The first problem one encounters in discussing the small firm sector in any country is that of defining what constitutes a small firm; there is an extraordinary variation across countries in this regard. In the UK the official definition of a small firm in manufacturing is one with less than 200 employees; in construction it is less than 25 employees, while in the service sector the definition is a turnover based one. This official definition for manufacturing (which has been much criticised as being too high) provides the basis of Table 5.5 which presents some relevant information on the size of the small firm sector in the UK.

The small firm sector in the UK is much less sizeable than that in other countries, such as Japan and West Germany, but the considerable academic and policy maker interest in it at the present time stems from the likelihood of current and future growth. This expectation of growth follows from the fact that, firstly, the rate of small business formation increases substantially in years of relatively high unemployment.(24) And secondly, the nature of government policies towards the small firm sector in the UK has changed quite noticeably from the late 1970s. A recent review of government policies towards small business which categorised them into the three groups of indirect asisstance, removal of discrimination and direct preferential assistance argued that the latter category had increased substantially in relative terms from the late 1970s.(25) And within this latter category itself there is evidence of an increased emphasis on direct financial measures, and on measures orientated towards new ventures relative to established small businesses. The position of the present Conservative Government with regard to the encouragement of small businesses is well known; the Department of Industry, for example, recently published a list of 98 measures designed specifically to assist small firms, ranging from the Loan Guarantee Scheme, under which the Government guarantees 80% of loans to small businesses from financial institutions, to the elimination of a good deal of form filling previously required by small firms.(26) The very considerable national, and local, level policy encouragement of the small firm sector in the UK at the present time should, however, be seen in the light of the following results, obtained from research in

131

Table 5.5: Small Firms in Manufacturing in the UK, 1970-1980

Year	Number of small enterprises (in thousands)	As % of all enterprises	Employment in small enterprises as % of total	Net output (by value) of small enterprises as % of total
1970	70.9	95.2	21.3	18.5
1971	71.4	95.3	21.0	17.9
1972	69.0	95.4	21.5	18.4
1973	74.1	95.7	20.7	17.1
1974	81.1	96.0	21.5	17.7
1975	83.4	96.3	21.9	18.0
1976	86.3	96.5	22.6	18.2
1977	86.7	96.6	22.5	18.7
1978	87.2	96.7	22.8	19.3
1979	86.8	96.8	23.1	19.5
1980	87.4	96.9	24.3	21.5

Source: James Curran and John Stanworth, 'Small Business Research in Britain', in Cyril Levicki (ed), Small Businesses: Theory and Policy, Croom Helm, London, 1984, p.148.

the North-East of England: (27)

(i)   at least 30% of new manufacturing businesses
        fail to survive for 4 years;
(ii)   the median level of employment of a wholly
        new business is 10 employees;
(iii)   the median new business shows no tendency
        to increase its employment after it has been
        established for 5 years;
(iv)   the probability of a wholly new business
        reaching 100 employees in a decade is
        between 0.5-0.75%;
(v)   there is no evidence of more rapid growth in
        the so-called 'high technology' sectors;
(vi)   4% of all new business starts created 34%
        of all employment in new firms.

These sorts of findings for potential
employment creation certainly seem to confirm
Cross's view that many of the arguments advanced
by policy makers for supporting small businesses
are more an article of faith than an established
fact.(28)   To Scase and Goffee the major reason
for the present Government's fostering of small
business is the Government's belief that this will
improve the management of labour, although their
own qualitative evidence, based on an extensive set
of interviews with small business owners, revealed
that one of the major fears and worries of such
owners concerns their ability to satisfactorily
manage labour.(29)   Specifically, they claim that
the desire and ability of many small businesses to
expand is frequently constrained by the belief
that this would undermine the informal and egalitarian work practices and arrangements favoured by
small businesses.   And that this would, in turn,
risk, among other things, the emergence of a trade
union presence in their organisations.   On the
question of trade unions, Scase and Goffee report
that small business owners typically feel that
unions are irrelevant to the present day working
environment (with individual employees already
having attained a sufficient set of protective
rights) and/or are a harmful force in the economy
at large, largely as a result of 'excessive'
political activities.   In this section we examine
a number of these contentions of Scase and Goffee,
using rather different sources of evidence to that
which they relied upon.

Non-Union Firms in the UK

The first set of evidence drawn upon here comes from a postal questionnaire conducted (with Barbara Townley of the University of Lancaster) in three new towns in the North-West of England (Central Lancashire, Skelmersdale and Warrington Runcorn). This study was very largely a replication of the work practices survey which was conducted in Scotland and reported on in the previous section. There were a number of reasons for conducting this survey in New Town locations. The first was that, as we saw in Chapter 1, the growth in manufacturing employment is increasingly taking place outside the large metropolitan centres of the UK. And secondly existing studies indicate that the employment growth of new towns is due more to their ability to attract new firms and plants than to the expansion of existing establishments.(30) This feature of new towns raises the possibility that any current employment growth there may be due to having attracted a 'new wave' of non-union plants and firms. Some discussion and evidence on this matter has already been presented for New Towns in Scotland so that here we have the opportunity to see whether this phenomenon is true of such locations south of the border.

The basic characteristics of the survey respondents in the three New Town locations in the North-West of England are set out below in Table 5.6.

Table 5.6: Basic Characteristics of Survey Respondents, North-West

% manufacturing sector	67
% US owned	10
% non-union	62
% single plant (in UK)	60
% established post-1976	77
mean size	42
total response	194
% response rate	25

Source: Beaumont and Townley, Loc.cit.

The major finding to emphasise here is the relatively high proportion of recently established plants which are in fact non-union; the latter figure is certainly not inconsistent with those reported earlier for the New Towns in Scotland. On the matter of work practices we found that, firstly, establishments in the North-West had, on

134

average, a lesser number than those in the Scottish
survey. And, secondly, non-union status was
significantly and negatively related (in contrast
to the Scottish survey) to the existence of a
relatively large number of work practices (i.e. 5 or
more). This difference from the Scottish survey
was due to the fact that non-union establishments
in the North-West New Towns were small, recently
established, single independent plants, with no
relationship with US ownership being apparent.

The major conclusions to be drawn from this
exercise were, firstly, the very limited extent of
overlap between the number and nature of work
practices in US owned and British owned non-union
establishments; this difference is essentially
attributable to the factors discussed in the
previous section. It was essentially the limited
US presence among the non-union establishments in
the North-West that explained the negative, as
opposed to positive (in Scotland) relationship with
the number of work practices; the small number of
US owned, non-union establishments in the North-
West survey (N = 9) did, however, have essentially
the same number of work practices as their counterparts in Scotland. In the North-West study the
only positive (as opposed to negative) relationship
between non-union status and the existence of a
particular work practice was with staff status;
this particular relationship was also apparent with
our British owned non-union establishments in
Scotland (see Table 5.4). In such small establishments staff status does not involve the formal,
negotiated set of arrangements typically discussed
in the relevant body of literature.(31) Instead
the strength and consistency of this finding in the
two surveys reflects Scase and Goffee's categori-
sation of an 'egalitarian' small business (as
opposed to a paternalist one) in which there is
much stress on the co-operative, team nature of the
enterprise, with employees being flexible and multi-
skilled.

The contents of Table 5.6 suggest that a
relatively high proportion of new, small businesses
is likely to be non-union. This particular
relationship (i.e. between non-union status and
small size) is, of course, well documented in the
existing literature; the 1980 workplace industrial
relations survey, for example, reported that only
44% of establishments with less than 50 employees
recognised manual unions compared to more than 90%

of establishments with more than 500 employees.(32)
The relative importance of the reasons or factors
behind this relationship remain, however, a matter
of some debate and disagreement among researchers.
The three separate, although not mutually exclusive,
reasons typically put forward to account for this
particular relationship are as follows:

(i)   union organisational constraints whereby
        financial and resource limitations make it
        not particularly cost effective to try and
        organise small firms;

(ii)   the relative absence of a bureaucratic
        working environment which limits any non-
        pecuniary job dissatisfaction among (the
        allegedly self selected group of) small firm
        employees which, in turn, limits any demand
        on their part for unionisation;

(iii)   the existence of relatively strong employer
        opposition to recognition, which typically
        takes the form of a union suppression (or
        in Bains terms, forcible opposition) as
        opposed to a union substitution (peaceful
        competition) approach.

The latter influence among these three is the
particular focus of the work which we now report on,
although, as we shall see, our empirical findings
appear to have some indirect bearing on the perceived influence of the other two factors.   It is
obviously difficult in practice to document the
tactics of forcible opposition to union recognition
on anything like a comprehensive basis so that the
approach adopted here is to try and identify the
sort of attitudes that one could expect to be associated with such an approach; in considering
attitudes we do, of course, acknowledge the possibility, particularly in changed circumstances,
that they may be a less than perfect guide to actual
patterns of behaviour.

However, before turning to our data it is
important to consider where any attitudes of union
opposition may have come from.   In Scase and
Goffee's study it was reported that the views of
small business founders that unions were too powerful and abused their position in society were
received and interpreted from secondary sources,
with few concrete examples being cited in support
of such beliefs.(33)   Alternatively, one can
consider the work of Schein who has explicitly
linked the founder role and the subsequent shape of

organisational culture.(34)   Unfortunately Schein's
observation that the ideas, values, attitudes etc.,
of the founder derive from (i) previous cultural
experiences and (ii) personality traits does not
take us very far being little more than a tautology
at this level of generalisation.   This reference
to 'previous cultural experiences' can, however, be
developed further in that the work of urban and
regional scholars in the UK has suggested that
persons establishing their own small businesses are
disproportionately likely to have an immediate
employment background in small sized plants;(35)
the reasons for this are typically held to be the
wide range of work experience (particularly customer
contact), the contact with other business founders
and the limited job security in such an environment.
This small plant background may, of course, be a
non-union one (for the reasons already given) which
raises, in turn, the possibility of them desiring
non-union status as a major component of any
organisational culture that they would wish to see
associated with their own firm;   we are, of course,
assuming here that this small plant background, if
non-union, has been a favourable, positive influence.   A desire for non-union status may in fact
extend beyond simply those founders coming from a
small, non-union plant background.   One hears, for
example, the inevitable stories of individuals who
have had 'bad experiences' in large, unionised
plants and, as a consequence, are insistent on non-
union status for their own businesses.   More
generally, existing small business research in the
UK has identified '... the stress placed on autonomy
and independence as major personal goals, with the
enterprise as the major arena for their expression.'(36)   These general sentiments in favour of
autonomy and independence could arguably manifest
themselves in a specific desire to minimise any
third party (e.g. trade union) involvement in the
workings of their organisation;   such sentiments
would certainly be consistent with Handy's discussion of a 'power culture' in organisations.(37)

     As was noted in Chapter 1, the determinants of
the owners (or senior management's) desire for non-
union status of their organisation has been the
subject of remarkably little systematic examination,
particularly in comparison with the attention given
to the influence on the employees'demand for unionisation.   The prevailing tendency in the literature
is simply to argue, on the basis of a few

illustrative examples, that the contemporary non-union status of an organisation reflects the value set of the original founders (or early period senior managers) of the organisation.   If this is in fact the case, and certainly much of the organisational culture literature would support it, then the current growth of new, small businesses in the UK provides an excellent opportunity to examine the factors that may be systematically associated with the original founder's desire for non-union status of the organisation.

An extensive search of the small firms litera-ture, the organisation culture literature, and that on entrepreneurship led us to produce the following list of hypotheses:

(i)   Those organisational founders who have reacted positively to an immediate employment background in a small, non-union establish-ment are particularly likely to desire non-union status for their own organisations;

(ii)   those organisational founders who have reacted negatively to an immediate employ-ment background in a large, unionised estab-lishment are particularly likely to desire non-union status for their own organisations;

(iii)   those organisational founders who have reacted positively to an immediate employ-ment background in the private services sector, with its limited tradition of work-force unionisation, are particularly likely to desire non-union status for their own organisations;

(iv)   those organisational founders who previously held managerial level positions and, as a consequence, are less likely to have been trade union members are particularly likely to desire non-union status for their own organisations;

(v)   those organisational founders who accord a particularly high priority to the achievement (through their organisation) of the personal goals of independence and autonomy are particularly likely to desire non-union status for their own organisations;

(vi)   those organisational founders who hold unfavourable views of the general role of trade unions in the economy and society at large are particularly likely to desire non-union status for their own organisations;

(vii)   those organisational founders who have reacted positively to an immediate employment background in a small, non-union establishment, but whose own organisation is in a different industry or area of economic activity may be particularly sensitive to, and aggressive in, trying to ensure non-union status for their own organisations;

(viii) those organisational founders whose expanding business involves a significant increase in workforce numbers may at such a time be particularly sensitive to, and aggressive in, trying to ensure non-union status for their organisations;

(ix)   those organisational founders experiencing a reduction in the organisation slack that has financed any discretionary employee benefits may at such a time be particularly sensitive to, and aggressive in, trying to ensure non-union status for their organisations.

These (and other possible) hypotheses are the sort of influences that need to be systematically examined given the available evidence in support of a growth in the number of small, single independent establishments in the UK. In a preliminary attempt to investigate the attitudes of (and influences on) small business founders with regard to trade unions, questionnaire responses were obtained (in work done with Ian Rennie at Bell College) from one hundred individuals who had typically been running their own small businesses for some 2-3 years. These persons had originally participated in Scottish Development Agency sponsored training courses for small businesses conducted at two colleges of further education in the Clydeside area, and consequently were members of the small business clubs associated with the two colleges. All of them had attended the Annual Meetings of the clubs in mid-1985, on which occasions the questionnaires were distributed, completed and returned. An assessment of the generality of our results must await further research involving individuals who have received no such formal training, or received it from different sources and who, most importantly of all, are situated in other regions and areas of the UK. At this stage we can simply caution against attempts to generate population estimates (with regard to the proportions holding particular attitudes) from our data and stress that our concern is with

whether any revealed attitudes are systematically
related to particular influences or factors (e.g.
a non-union plant employment background).

The basic responses to individual questions
about certain aspects of unionisation are summarised
below in Table 5.7.

Table 5.7: Responses to Questions on Unionisation,
            Small Business Founders

Prior plant of employment was non-union	34%
Never been a member of a trade union	38%
Own business is not unionised	85%
Trade union recognition of own business is felt to be extremely unlikely or unlikely in next 5 years	67%
Trade union recognition of own business would be viewed as extremely unhelpful or unhelpful to effective operation	41%
Agreed extremely strongly or strongly with statement that unions in general were too powerful	42%
Agreed extremely strongly or strongly with statement that unions had damaged the economic performance of the UK	59%

An examination was then made of the existence
(or not) of any systematic influences on (i) current
recognition status, (ii) those saying recognition
was extremely unlikely or unlikely and (iii) those
saying recognition would be extremely unhelpful
or unhelpful to organisational performance.   This
exercise involved an examination via correlation
analysis of a number of the previously listed hypotheses.   In fact, we estimated the following basic
model:

(i)   Personal and demographic characteristics.
Here we considered the possible influence of sex,
age (less than 30 versus the rest) and whether the
founder had ever been a member of a trade union.
(ii) Immediate employment background.   Here we
considered the possible influence of previous job
level (managerial versus the rest), establishment
size (less than 25 employees versus the rest),
sector of employment (private sector services versus
the rest), and whether the previous establishment
recognised trade unions.

(iii) <u>Characteristics of own business</u>.   Here we considered the possible influence of establishment size (more than 10 employees versus the rest), and sector of employment (private sector services versus the rest).

(iv)   <u>Attitudes towards unions in general</u>.   Here we considered the possible influence of attitudes or beliefs that unions were too powerful and had damaged the economic performance of the UK.

The correlation coefficients obtained are listed in Table 5.8.

In a preliminary exercise of this type the number of significant correlations was encouraging, while the fact that the pattern of significance varied across the three issues examined was both pleasing and interesting.   As regards current recognition, the contents of Table 5.8 indicate that this was associated with a founder who had previously worked in a unionised establishment, did not hold the view that unions were generally too powerful and had a relatively larger sized organ-isation.   Those founders who viewed union recog-nition in their organisation as either unlikely or extremely unlikely were female, aged below 30, had not been a union member themselves, had previously worked in an establishment that was in the service sector and did not recognise unions, and whose own organisations were in the service sector.   Younger age, a non-union establishment and private sector services background were also associated with founders who viewed the prospect of recognition as unhelpful or extremely unhelpful to the performance of their organisations.   In addition, a small establishment background, a belief that unions were generally too powerful, and their own organisations in the private sector were all associated with this particular view of the prospect of trade union recognition.

As a result of this preliminary exercise being undertaken on a relatively small sized sample (with considerable multi-collinearity present) it was felt that correlation analysis was a more appropri-ate method of analysis than that of multiple regres-sion.   A number of multiple and stepwise regress-ion estimates were nevertheless undertaken, the basic results of which are worthy of brief note. Firstly, the level of overall explanatory power achieved by the three sets of estimates (R^2 of 0.17-0.21) were not unreasonable for cross-section equations based on individuals as the unit

Table 5.8: The Correlations Between Listed Independent Variables and Various Aspects of Recognition, Small Business Founders

	(i) Current Recognition (=1)	(ii) Recognition unlikely or extremely unlikely (=1)	(iii) Recognition unhelpful or extremely unhelpful (=1)
Sex (male =1)	0.156	-0.176*	-0.112
Age (V 30 = 1)	-0.100	0.188*	0.246**
Trade union member (yes = 1)	0.098	-0.190*	-0.080
Previous job level (managerial = 1)	0.106	-0.144	-0.144
Previous sized establishment (<25 = 1)	-0.022	0.055	-0.172*
Sector of previous employment establishment (private services sector = 1)	-0.067	0.168*	0.275***
Previous establishment recognised unions (yes = 1)	0.214**	-0.190*	-0.190*
Size of own business (>10 = 1)	0.276***	-0.079	-0.085
Sector of own business (private services sector = 1)	-0.075	0.249**	0.194*
Belief that unions are too powerful (=1)	-0.187*	0.115	0.223**
Belief that unions damaged the economic performance of the UK economy (=1)	0.009	0.053	0.056

* significant at 0.10 level ** significant at 0.05 level *** significant at 0.01 level

of observation.   Secondly, the significance of
individual variables was far from robust in the
estimates of the likelihood of recognition, whereas
in the estimates for current recognition and the
prospect of recognition being unhelpful or extremely
unhelpful a number of individual variables remained
consistently significant;   these particular variables were size of own organisation and view of
union power in the current recognition case, and
private sector services background and view of union
power in the case of the estimates for recognition
would be unhelpful or extremely unhelpful.
      As well as the need for further survey based
research to more fully test the sort of hypotheses
considered here, one could utilise the semi-
structured interview approach of Scase and Goffee
to try and identify the particular behaviour and
tactics that might be particularly associated with
union opposition in the small firm sector.   One
recent study has, for example, suggested that small
firm founders may respond to an employee interest
in union recognition with a threat to close or re-
locate the plant.(38)   This particular matter was
explored in a series of interviews and discussions
conducted with some 10 small business founders in
the Clydeside area.   Although some sympathy was
expressed with such action ('one can easily understand it occurring'), the vast majority of the
interviewees did not view this as a sensible
strategy.   This was not so much because it was
viewed as being outwith the 'rules of the game',
but rather because it was held to be 'giving in' to
the unions, throwing away years of effort and work
by the owner and risking the loss of reputation
with local area customers.   The reasons for
rejecting this particular response when taken in
conjunction with a number of other comments led us
to conclude that, unlike 'the leaders of very
large businesses (who) are obliged to take special
cognizance of their economic, social and sometimes
political prominence'(39), 'image management' will
play very little role in shaping the nature of
small firm responses to demands for union recognition.

Conclusions
This chapter has reviewed a number of pieces of
evidence which suggest that a relatively high
proportion of recently established firms, particularly in locations such as New Towns, are non-

union establishments.   These were not the US
owned, high technology establishments that have
figured so prominently in popular discussion.
Rather, they were overwhelmingly British owned,
single independent establishments of relatively
small size.   In terms of their implications for
the future level of union density in the UK
attention is typically given to their relatively
small size.   A fact that should equally be
stressed is that of single, independent status.
This follows from some of Daniel and Millward's
work which indicated that at private sector establishments employing fewer than 10 non-manual
workers, only 2% of independent establishments
recognised non-manual unions compared with 36%
of their size counterparts in larger organisations.(40)   The point here is that if the population of establishments in an individual local
labour market, region, or the country as a whole
has an increased proportion of single independent
establishments then this tendency is one that
does not favour union recognition.

In such establishments employee relations
tended to be viewed by the founders as essentially
involving good informal communications and flexible
working practices, with relatively little need
being perceived for technical advice or the
emulation of practices in larger sized establishments.   Specifically, we found relatively little
evidence of an overlap between the working practices
of US and British owned non-union establishments.
Accordingly, if the former, as well as the household name non-union firms in the UK, are acting as
opinion leaders it is not among these particular
establishments that they are exerting an influence,
at least not at this initial start-up stage.

In this chapter mention was made of the present
Government's desire to encourage the development
of these particular firms.   The next two chapters
more fully explore the Government's intentions to
stimulate and facilitate change in the 'non-union'
direction, by considering the Government roles of
employer and legislator respectively.

NOTES

1.   David Deaton, "Management and Industrial
Relations", Unpublished Report of the Workplace
Industrial Relations Survey, December 1981,
(mimeographed)

2.   W.W. Daniel and Neil Millward, Workplace
Industrial Relations in Britain, Heinemann, London,
1983, pp.257-259.
3.   Derek Norman, "How a New Plant Made
Pilkington Reflect on its IR Structure", Personnel
Management, Vol.15, No.8, August 1983, p.22.
4.   D.J. Storey, "The Problems Facing New
Firms", Journal of Management Studies, Vol.22, No.3,
1985, pp.327-345.
5.   Andrew Gould and David Kebble, "New Firms
and Rural Industrialisation in East Anglia",
Regional Studies, Vol.18, No.3, 1984, pp.187-199.
6.   Daniel and Millward, op.cit., p.31. (Also
the figures in Chapter 4 here.)
7.   Tony Lane, "The Unions Caught on an Ebb
Tide", Marxism Today, Vol.26, No.9, September 1982,
p.9.
8.   J. Storey, The Challenge of Management
Control, Business Books, London, 1980.
9.   Daniel and Millward, op.cit., pp.197-199.
10.   Antone Aboud (ed), Plant Closing Legislation, Key Issues, No.27, ILR Press, Cornell
University, 1984, p.50.
11.   This section draws heavily on Nicholas
Newman, "Britain's Non-Union Leaders", Management
Today, July 1980.
12.   Roy J. Lewicki, "Organisational Seduction,
Building Commitment to Organisations", Organisational Dynamics, Autumn 1981, p.7.
13.   ACAS, Employment Protection Act 1975,
Section 12, Report No.44, July 1977, pp.10-11.
14.   Sunday Times, 30th October 1971.
15.   Neil Hood and Stephen Young, Multinationals in Retreat: The Scottish Experience,
Edinburgh University Press, Edinburgh, 1982, p.5.
16.   SDA, Labor Performance of US Plants in
Scotland, 1984, p.11.
17.   East Kilbride: A Labour Study, East
Kilbride Development Corporation, 1982, p.7.
18.   L. Cairns, "Non-Union Establishments in
New Towns in Scotland", Unpublished M.Phil in
Industrial Relations Dissertation, University of
Glasgow, 1985.
19.   Thomas A. Kochan and Michael J. Piore,
"Will the New Industrial Relations Last? Implications for the American Labor Movement", The Annals
of the American Academy of Political Science, No.473
May 1984, p.183.
20.   Tom Burns and G.M. Stalker, The Management
of Innovation, Tavistock Publications, London, 1959.

21.   V.V. Murray and D.E. Dimick, "Contextual Influences on Personnel Policies and Programs: An Explanatory Model", Academy of Management Review, October 1978, p.756.
22.   Murray and Dimick, op.cit., p.757.
23.   Peter Cressey, "Recasting Collectivism: Non-Unionisation in Two American Branch Plants", paper given to the Conference on "The Role of Trade Unions in the Coming Decade", Maastricht, November 1985.
24.   Stephen Fothergill and Graham Gudgin, Unequal Growth, Heinemann, London, 1982, pp.117-119.
25.   M. Beesley and P. Wilson, "Government Aid to the Small Firm Since Bolton", in J. Stanworth et al (eds) Perspectives on a Decade of Small Business Research, Gower, Aldershot, 1982, pp.181-199.
26.   James Curran and John Stanworth, "Small Business Research in Britain", in Cyril Levicki (ed), Small Business Theory and Policy, Croom Helm, London, 1984, pp.144-145.
27.   D.J. Storey, "Regional Policy in a Recession", National Westminster Bank Quarterly Review, November 1983, pp.44-45.
28.   Michael Cross, "The United Kingdom", in D. Storey (ed), The Small Firm: An International Survey, Croom Helm, London, 1983, pp.84-119.
29.   R. Scase and R. Goffee, The Real World of the Small Business Owner, Croom Helm, London, 1980.
30.   Robert A. Henderson, "The Employment Performance of Established Manufacturing Industry in the Scottish New Towns", Urban Studies, Vol.21, No.3, August 1984, pp.295-316.
31.   Alan Arthurs, "Egalitarianism in the Workplace?" in Valerie Hammond (ed) Current Research on Management, Pinter, London, 1985, pp.130-145.
32.   Daniel and Millward, ibid., p.22.
33.   Scase and Goffee, op.cit., pp.115-118.
34.   Edgar H. Schein, "The Role of the Founder in Creating Organizational Culture", Organizational Dynamics, Summer 1983, pp.13-28.
35.   Fothergill and Gudgin, op.cit., pp.125-126
36.   Curran and Stanworth in Levicki (ed) op.cit., p.134.
37.   Charles Handy, Understanding Organizations, Penguin, Harmondsworth, 1985, pp.188-190.
38.   Patrick Gunnigle and Therese Brady, "The Management of Industrial Relations in the Small Firm", Employee Relations, Vol.6, No.5, 1984, p.21.

39. Peter J.A. Herbert (Appendix) in Walter Goldsmith and David Clutterbuck _The Winning Streak_, 1984, p.181.
40. Daniel and Millward, _ibid._, p.53.

Chapter Six

THE PUBLIC SECTOR EXPERIENCE AND EXAMPLE

In any national system of industrial relations the
government of the day has two potential means of
influencing the level of union organisation.   The
first is via legislation, while the second is
through the treatment of its own employees in the
public sector which can, in turn, constitute a
'leadership by example' model for the private
sector.   The first of these routes is considered
in Chapter 7, while the second is the concern of
the present chapter.

        The whole of the 1970s witnessed Governments
of both political persuasions in the UK coming into
open conflict with public sector unions as they
struggled to reconcile their responsibility for
macro-economic management with that for the well-
being of their own employees.   Throughout that
decade, public sector unions continually claimed
that the Government of the day had dishonoured
their traditional commitment to act as a good
employer of labour by seeking to enforce the
restrictions of incomes policies most vigorously on
their own employees.   However, the present Conservative Government is held to have moved well
beyond the position of making ad hoc attempts to
limit the size of public sector wage increases to
one of actually questioning and constraining the
institutional role of trade unions in the public
sector.

        Given this book's particular focus on the level
of trade union organisation the three most relevant
initiatives of the present Government to be discussed here are the privatisation moves, the repeal
of the Fair Wages Resolution and the union decertification at GCHQ.   A recent review of the latter
episode explicitly raised the question of whether
this might not act to encourage employers in the

148

private sector to withdraw union recognition;(1) the decertification of the Professional Air Traffic Controllers Organisation by the Reagan Administration following the 1981 strike is certainly alleged to have had this sort of influence in the United States. This possibility is obviously difficult to examine on a systematic basis, although the concluding section of the chapter does draw together some available evidence on decertification tendencies in the UK.

These particular initiatives of the present Government need to be set in the context of a larger view of public sector industrial relations. One such view is provided by Hepple who has outlined a traditional model (which was operative, in his view, roughly speaking between 1919 and 1970) and a new emerging model.(2) The latter consists of five basic features: (i) the transformation of the sovereign employer ideology; (ii) the decline of the principle of comparability with the private sector; (iii) the demise of the government as a model employer; (iv) the pressure for decentralisation of rule making; and (v) the development of circumscribed collective bargaining. The material to be presented in this chapter generally fits under feature (iii) where Hepple has claimed that it has been '... deliberate policy, since 1979, of taking government off its pedestal as a model for progressive labour relations policies ...'(3) The other features of the new model of public sector industrial relations are largely outwith the general concern of the book, and hence this chapter, although some of our subsequent material will obviously have some bearing on them.

The Traditional Encouragement of Unionisation
The actual meaning (and implications) of the government acting as a model (or good) employer of labour have not always been spelled out explicitly. However, one such attempt is contained in the following extract from the Priestley Report on the Civil Service:(4)

> The 'good employer' is not necessarily the one who offers the highest rates of pay. He seeks rather to provide stability and continuity of employment, and consults with representatives of his employees upon changes that affect both their remuneration and their conditions of work. He provides adequate facilities for training and advancement and

carries on a range of practices which today
constitute good management ... Such employers
are likely to be among the more progressive
in all aspects of management.

Among the traditional, tangible expressions of
this obligation in the public sector have been the
active encouragement of union organisation among
employees, the payment of 'above average' wages,
extensive joint consultation arrangements, early,
well developed disciplinary/dismissal procedures
and a willingness to experiment with new forms of
working practices and arrangements. The degree
of application of this concept has never, however,
lacked its critics. For example, the disprop-
tionate number of low paid workers in the public
sector is often held to be inconsistent with this
good employer obligation. On the other hand, there
have been suggestions that the 'excessive' job
security of public sector employees is the result
of taking this obligation too far. Most importantly of all is the long standing question of
whether this particular employer obligation
logically implies an awkward quid pro quo for public
sector unions in an adverse macro-economic environment, i.e. gains in good times have to be offset
against losses (to set an example of restraint to
the private sector) in tough times. In fact one
could disagree somewhat with Hepple's view that the
present Government has sought to move away from
providing a role model for private sector employers.
One can certainly agree with him that it has
departed from the traditional role model, but this
should not be taken to mean that it is not trying
to set some sort of example to the private sector;
recall here the earlier observation regarding GCHQ
and decertification tendencies. In other words,
the example setting role may remain (and indeed be
enhanced), but rather it is the nature of the
example being set that has changed.

What has never been in doubt is that, firstly,
the Government has traditionally encouraged union
organisation among its employees and, secondly,
that the public sector is, and has been for some
considerable time, the most highly unionised part
of the economy. On the first matter, the Civil
Service staff handbook, for example, has traditionally urged all new employees to join staff representative organisations on the grounds that 'the
existence of fully representative associations not
only promotes good staff relations but is essential

to effective negotiation of conditions of service'.(5)   And, as we saw in Chapter 1, the figures
of Price and Bain indicated that union density in
the public sector in 1979 was nearly 83%, compared
to figures of some 69% and 17% in manufacturing
and private sector services respectively.   One of
the most distinctive features of the high level of
union organisation in the public sector is just how
far such organisation extends up the employment
hierarchy, penetrating well into the managerial and
executive grades that are relatively little
organised in the private sector.   Although, as we
shall discuss in the next chapter, union density and
collective bargaining coverage are far from synonymous terms in the UK the figures for the latter in
Table 6.1 are worthy of note.

The contents of Table 6.1 indicate that the
extent of collective agreement coverage in the
public sector is substantially in excess of that
in the private sector for all eight socio-economic
groupings listed.   Moreover, for most of the
groups in the public sector bargaining coverage is
little short of 100%.

The role of the government in encouraging
these relatively high levels of union density and
collective bargaining coverage has been questioned
in two different ways.   The first line of criticism is that the relatively high union density of
the public sector is ultimately attributable more
to employment being concentrated in relatively
large sized establishments, with their highly
bureaucratic working arrangements than to this
employer encouragement.(6)   A second, and quite
different, criticism is that such encouragement has
adversely affected the character of many public
sector unions, making them 'less protest bodies
than administrative unions...'(7)   The contention
here is that a sizeable number of public sector
specific unions, particularly in education, the
NHS and the civil service, would, in Blackburn's
term, be relatively low on unionateness.(8)   This
latter view and criticism has, however, receded
from the 1970s as many of these unions began to
exhibit attitudes and behaviour (e.g. strikes,
affiliation to the TUC), markedly different from
their historical patterns.

In Chapter 1 we suggested that the level of
union density in the public sector was so high by
the late 1970s that there was the possibility of a
saturation effect.   That is, a further increase

Table 6.1: Collective Bargaining Coverage in Public and Private Sectors, Males, 1978

Socio-Economic Groupings	Sector	Percentage covered by collective bargaining for wage purposes
Managers	Public	90.7
	Private	26.7
Professionals	Public	93.8
	Private	34.3
Intermediate non-manuals	Public	96.7
	Private	37.7
Junior non-manuals	Public	97.7
	Private	46.7
Foremen	Public	94.8
	Private	60.3
Skilled manuals	Public	96.1
	Private	73.3
Semi-skilled manuals	Public	96.6
	Private	67.8
Unskilled manuals	Public	96.9
	Private	67.3

Source: M.B. Gregory and A.W.J. Thomson, 'The Coverage Mark Up, Bargaining Structure and Earnings in Britain, 1973, 1978', British Journal of Industrial Relations, Vol.XIX, No.1, March 1981, p.28.

in union density (as opposed to one in union membership) could only be obtained by an inordinate investment of effort and resources on the union's part. The present Government's stated intention of 'rolling back the public sector' also raises questions about the absolute number of union members in the public sector. Accordingly, before turning to consider the specific initiatives involving privatisation, the repeal of the Fair Wages Resolution and union decertification at GCHQ, the next section briefly reviews changes in public sector employment in recent years.

Recent Changes in Public Sector Employment
In mid-1984 an estimated 6.8 million (28.5%) members of the UK workforce were in the public sector. This total consisted of 1.6 million (6.7%) in public corporations, 2.3 million (9.7%) in central government and 2.9 million (12%) in

local government.   According to a recent article
in <u>Economic Trends</u>, public sector employment reached
its peak in 1979, since when (to mid-1984) the
following changes have occurred:(5)

(i)   in total public sector employment declined
         by 7.9% on a headcount basis and 8.8% in
         full-time equivalents (the transfer of
         British Telecom to the private sector in
         November 1984 adds over 3% to these figures);
(ii)   employment in the NHS increased by 6.1% on
         a full-time equivalent basis, and by 6.2%
         in numbers;
(iii)   other central government employment fell by
         11.6% on a head count basis, and rather more
         in full-time equivalents;
(iv)   local authority employment fell by a little
         under 4% on both bases.

     The picture that emerges here is clearly one
of considerable variation in the extent of employment change in the different parts of the public
sector.   Compare, for example, the employment
fall of 22% in public corporations in 1978-1984
with the 9% increase for the NHS while in local
authorities education fell by 5.4% whereas both
social services and the police showed a 10%
increase.   The case of the civil service is
particularly worthy of consideration given that the
present Government entered office with the explicit
aim of reducing the size of the civil service from
732,000 to 630,000 posts by April 1984;   a 14%
reduction in staffing over a 5 year period.   In
fact the Government more than achieved this target,
with the civil service being down to 623,972 in
April 1984;   a 14.8% reduction.   This over-
achievement of the target led the Government to
announce (in November 1983) their intention to seek
a further 6% reduction of the civil service in the
following four years.   The reductions achieved
in the 1979-1984 period were estimated to have come
about in the following ways:(10)

(i)   increased efficiency after changes in work
         practices: approximately 55%
(ii)   cutting back or dropping functions:
         approximately 20%
(iii)   privatisation, including contracting out:
         10%
(iv)   hiving off to new or existing public sector
         bodies: 2%
(These figures do not add to 100% because of
workload changes.)

153

In Table 6.2 we set out the reductions achieved
(1979-1984) and targeted reductions (1984-1988) for
individual departments in the civil service.
The contents of Table 6.2 indicate considerable
variation in the degree of change between individual
departments. Four of the 15 departments (or
groupings) listed actually show increases for the
period 1979-1984, while the size of the reduction
varied from a high of 34% to a low of 7% in these
years. The reductions achieved to date have been
largely through natural wastage, retirement and
redeployment. There appear to have been relatively
few instances of redundancies. The years 1979-
1984 saw 3,200 redundancies in the non-industrial
grades and 14,700 among industrial civil servants
(approximately a half of the latter occurred in
1983); redundancies only accounted for 0.2, 1.1
and 0.8 per cent of all leavers in the non-
industrial civil service in 1979, 1982 and 1983
respectively.(11) Outwith the civil service, the
scale of redundancies appears to have been considerably greater. For example, a survey, which
was conducted at the University of Glasgow, of some
45% of all local authorities found that some 70%
of these had made employees redundant. These were
overwhelmingly voluntary or induced redundancies
as some two-thirds of the respondent authorities
stated that they had a declared policy of avoiding
compulsory redundancies.
In view of these changes in public sector
employment it is hardly surprising that strikes
(and other forms of industrial action) have occurred
over manpower, redundancy, manning etc., issues.
The general frequency of such action should not,
however, be exaggerated. A recent survey of union
branches in the public sector, for example, found
that redundancy was a relatively infrequent
occurrence compared to changes in hours and the
freezing of vacancies and, as a consequence, there
had been little in the way of negotiation over and
opposition (in the form of industrial action) to,
what they termed 'job erosion'.(12) Nevertheless,
an examination of the prominent stoppages (i.e.
those involving more than 5,000 working days lost)
recorded by the Department of Employment for the
years 1976-1983 revealed that the public sector
accounted for nearly 50% of the prominent redundancy
disputes in 1980-1983 compared to less than 15%
in the period 1976-1979. These prominent manpower
disputes, as well as the various national wage
strikes that have occurred (steel in 1980, the

Table 6.2: Civil Service Employment Change, Actual and Proposed, by Departments

	1 April 1979	1 April 1984	% change 1979-84	target 1 April 1988	% change 1984-88
Defence	247,000	200,000	-19	170,000	-15
Energy	1,300	1,100	-15	1,000	- 9
Treasury, Inland Revenue, Customs & Excise etc.	126,900	113,000	-11	104,200	- 8
Employment, Manpower Services Commission, etc.	53,700	57,700	+ 7	54,000	- 6
Environment	56,000	37,000	-34	34,600	- 6
Foreign Office	12,000	11,200	- 7	10,500	- 6
Health and Social Security	98,400	90,700	- 8	87,900	- 3
Scottish Office	10,900	9,800	-10	9,500	- 3
Agriculture	14,000	11,500	-18	11,300	- 2
Education	2,600	2,400	- 8	2,400	nil
Trade and Industry	19,500	14,900	-24	14,900	nil
Transport	13,900	14,200	+ 2	14,200	nil
Welsh Office	2,600	2,200	-15	2,200	nil
Courts, etc.	16,500	17,300	+ 5	17,400	+1
Home Office	33,500	35,800	+ 7	41,100	+15
All Civil Service	732,300	624,000	-15	592,700	- 6

N.B. Total includes small departments not listed separately

Source: David Thomas, 'Honing Down the Civil Service', New Society, 17th January 1985.

civil service in 1981, the NHS in 1982 and the water
supply industry in 1983) as relative wage changes
have moved against the public sector from 1981-1982,
are clearly important in accounting for the fact
that the public sector has contributed a disproportionate amount of the total working days lost
through strike activity in the UK since 1979.   The
obvious case in point here is the miners' action of
1984-1985 which involved some 26 million working
days lost, the highest in any industry since 1926.
And, as a result, the total number of working days
lost through strike activity in 1984 was the second
highest (after 1979) since the war.
    What is the future of public sector employment?
The detailed employment estimates of the Institute
of Employment Research (at the University of
Warwick) for the years 1985-1990 (in '000s) are as
follows:(13)

Agriculture	-58
Mining	0
Manufacturing	-78
Construction	143
Public utilities	-20
Private services	379
Public services	245
	610

    There is certainly an expectation of net new
jobs being created in public services, although the
numbers involved are considerably less than in the
private services sector;   in fact, as mentioned in
an earlier chapter, the latter is estimated to
account for nearly 66% of the total number of net
new jobs in this period of time, a fact that does
not augur well for the maintenance of overall union
density.

Some Union Membership Figures
As we saw in Chapter 1, sectoral or industry based
estimates of union density are not, as yet,
available for the years since 1979.   However,
comments in, for example, the Annual Reports of
ACAS, lead us to believe that union density has not
noticeably declined among those in employment in
the public sector from that time.   There have,
nevertheless, been some notable changes in the
membership figures of individual unions in the
public sector.   The contents of Table 6.3 indicate
the direction and extent of reported membership

change in the years 1979-1984 for the unions listed.
      The table lists 16 unions, with only 6 of
these showing recorded membership increases in
1979-1984.   The extent of the gains for these six
were NALGO (1.7%), NAS/UWT (3.3%), FBU (2.4%),
COHSE (0.5%), RCN (42.6%) and NCU (31.8%).   The
dramatic growth of the Royal College of Nursing
obviously stands out here; in fact the RCN, which
only recruits qualified nurses, grew to such an
extent that by 1983 it was larger than its main
rival COHSE (an all grades union for the health
service), for the first time ever.   A major reason
for the few unions in the public sector that
recorded membership increases in these years is
the essential absence of union amalgamations there.
In this regard John Lloyd recently noted that fully
22 of the 25 leading unions to record membership
increases in 1984/1985 - 1985/1986 had done so
through amalgamations.(14)   And such amalgamations have been much more a private than a public
sector phenomenon.   The notable merger in the
public sector was the National Communications Union
with a membership of 160,000 which came into being
in February 1985 as a result of the merger of POEU
with the post and telecommunications group of CPSA.
The proposed merger between CPSA and SCPS failed
to come about, however, due to its rejection at the
former's annual conference in 1985.
      Against this general background we now turn to
consider the three specific initiatives of the
present Government which would appear to constitute
the most direct threat to the level of union
organisation in the public sector.   These are the
privatisation moves, the repeal of the Fair Wages
Resolution and the union decertification at GCHQ.

The Moves Towards Privatisation
In discussing such moves it is essential to specify
just what we are talking about.   This is because
'privatisation is a new word, scarcely heard before
1979, which has quickly gained popular currency as
an umbrella term for very many different policies,
loosely linked by the way in which they are taken
to mean a strengthening of the market at the
expense of the state'.(15)   According to Heald
there are in fact four separate components of the
term 'privatisation':(16)

Table 6.3: Trade Unions in the Public Sector, Membership Figures (thousands) 1979-1984

	1979	1980	1981	1982	1983	1984
CENTRAL GOVERNMENT						
CPSA	224	216	209	199	191	150
SCPS	108	109	101	96	93	86
LOCAL GOVERNMENT						
NALGO	753	782	796	784	780	766
NUPE	692	699	704	702	689	673
NUT	249	232	224	222	210	214
NAS/UWT	122	124	120	120	120	126
FBU	42	41	42	43	43	43
NHS						
COHSE	213	216	231	232	223	214
RCN	162	181	197	223	231	N/A
TRADING SECTOR						
ISTC	110	104	103	95	93	79
NUM	253	257	250	245	208	200
NUR	170	167	157	150	143	136
ASLEF	27	27	26	25	24	23
TSSA	N/A	70	67	60	56	49
UCW	203	203	202	198	196	195
NCU	126	131	133	137	130	166

Sources: Report of the Certification Officer 1979-1984 supplemented by TUC Annual Reports 1979-1985.

(i)   privatisation of the financing of a service (through an increased role of charges relative to taxes) which continues to be produced by the public sector;

(ii)   privatisation of the production of a service (through contracting out work to the private sector) which continues to be financed by the public sector out of taxation;

(iii)   denationalisation and load shedding, meaning respectively the selling off of public enterprises and the transfer of hitherto state functions to the private sector;

(iv)   liberalisation, meaning a relaxation of any statutory monopolies or licensing arrangements which prevent private sector firms from entering markets previously exclusively supplied by the public sector.

There have been a variety of arguments advanced by advocates of such privatisation moves, among these being the desire to weaken the power of public sector unions. This weakening could take a variety of forms, including reduced collective bargaining coverage, the break-up of national level bargaining (the results of relative wage studies, which control for bargaining structure, would not suggest this change involves a weakening of the unions) and an increased wage elasticity of demand for labour.(17) With the privatisation programme in its relative infancy it is not, as yet, possible to identify the existence of any changes along these lines. However, as an indication of the nature of Government thinking on such matters it is useful to consider the case of the 1983 Water Act. This Act, which was passed against the background of a threatened national strike in the water industry, reconstituted the institutional structure on which the industry was based, substituting small executive authorities for the much larger authorities consisting mainly of local authority nominees, established by the Water Act 1973; it was a highly controversial measure with many complaints of a likely reduction in public accountability. As well as abolishing the National Water Council, the legislation resulted in the 5 national negotiating bodies covering pay and conditions in the industry being wound up. The Government was in favour of completely abolishing national pay bargaining in the newly re-organised industry. However, some national

arrangements were retained with 4 new national
negotiating bodies (for manuals, craft, staff, chief
and senior officers) being created.   Their
constitutions limit them to deal with pay and main
conditions of service, with some items (e.g.
subsistence allowances) to be solely negotiated
at the individual employer level.   Other significant changes to previous arrangements include the
non-renewal of the post entry closed shop and the
removal of the unilateral right to arbitration.
The future of closed shop arrangements in other
parts of the public sector (e.g. British Rail) is
also in doubt, while a Department of Employment
Report in 1981 recommended that public sector
management withdraw from and renegotiate all
arrangements providing for unilateral arbitration,
which the report viewed as favouring the union
side.(18)

There is a slowly accumulating body of evidence
on the extent of privatisation moves in the
different parts of the public sector.   For example,
the local authorities survey, which was referred
to earlier, found that 31% of the respondent
authorities had sought tenders for privatisation
in manual grade areas (16% in APTC grades), while
23% had actually privatised services in the manual
grades (12% in the APTC grades).   A recent review
of the first 2 years of privatisation in the NHS in
England and Wales reported that in the area of
hospital catering the private sector only won 5 out
of 33 contracts put out to tender between 1983-1985
and one of these has since returned in-house.(19)
The catering contractors, organised through the
British Hotels, Restaurants and Caterers Association, have argued that the rules are weighted in
favour of the in-house tender and that the timescale
the DHSS was forcing on health authorities meant
that the private sector could not cope with the
workload.   The Government has recently brought in
management consultants to review the situation.
On the cleaning side private contractors have won
some 70% of the contracts already awarded, saving
the NHS an estimated £9.2 million.   There have
been a number of strikes against privatisation in
the NHS (particularly protracted ones occurring in
Barking, Hammersmith and Cambridge) and the ACAS
Annual Report for 1984 indicates a number of
conciliation exercises over such matters.

These privatisation moves have clearly
pressured a number of public sector unions to seek
rule changes to their constitutions permitting them
160

to recruit members in the private sector.) The
NCU, for example, have stated their intention to
increase the recruitment of information technology
workers outside British Telecom, something that
their constitution (previously POEU) prohibited
prior to 1981. NALGO have estimated that their
membership is likely to peak at around 800,000 and
then decline as a result of public expenditure cuts,
the introduction of new technology and privatisation
initiatives. This assessment led to the 1983
Annual Conference debating a proposed rule change
to allow them to recruit in the private sector.
On that occasion the motion was defeated, largely
as a result of arguments to the effect that it
would undermine the union's opposition to privatisation and was contrary to the longer term aim of
industrial unionism. At the 1984 Annual Conference
the motion was re-introduced, with the necessary
two-thirds majority support being received on this
occasion. From the individual union point of view
such a change has considerable logic and appeal.
However, if the result is an increase in the extent
and intensity of inter-union competition there are
some possible dangers for the position of the union
movement as a whole. These include the 'splitting
of employee votes' which we observed in our analysis
of the outcome of white collar recognition claims
(in Chapter 3), as well as increased pressure on
the minimal level of terms and conditions in procedural agreements.

The Repeal of the Fair Wages Resolution

The Fair Wages Resolution of the House of Commons
obliged government contractors to recognise the
right of employees to be union members and to
receive the appropriate industry wage. The first
such resolution was passed in 1891 in the context
of public concern over the sweated labour system.
This resolution was superseded by a second one in
1909, which was in turn replaced by the third and
final resolution of 1946. The principle underlying
these resolutions was that the government had a duty
to use its bargaining power as a contracting party
to ensure that other employers observed at least
certain minimum standards of fairness in their
terms and conditions of employment. The 1946
resolution constituted the final step in establishing a close connection between the concept of 'fair
wages' and the terms and conditions of collective
agreements, i.e. the outcome of the collective
bargaining process became explicitly acknowledged

as the relevant standard of 'fairness' to be met
by the contractors' terms and conditions of employment.   In other words, although the basic aim of
these resolutions was to eliminate unfair wage
competition among government contractors, they
also sought to influence more generally the development of union organisation and collective bargaining.   Indeed it had been a tacit hope of many
supporters of this particular policy instrument that
these sorts of indirect effects would be of even
greater significance than the achievement of the
direct objectives. (20)

The Fair Wages Resolution was also embodied
in certain Acts of Parliament covering industries
in receipt of government grants, loans or subsidies.
In addition many local authorities voluntarily
adopted fair wages clauses in their dealings with
private sector contractors; our local authorities
survey (conducted in 1982) found that more than 75%
of the respondents made use of such clauses.
What is the likely impact of the Government's
rescission of this resolution, with effect from
21 September 1983 (this necessitated denouncing
ILO Convention 94)?   In seeking to answer this
question one needs to consider the historical track
record of the resolution.

There has in fact been a great deal of success
claimed for the workings of these resolutions; one
of Britain's most distinguished industrial relations
scholars has gone so far as to claim that 'it can
be said with confidence that, to some extent, it
is this system of fair wages clauses which accounts
for the functioning in this country of voluntary
collective bargaining without legal sanctions'. (21)
There are in practice considerable difficulties in
trying to fully assess the impact and value of these
resolutions.   An examination of their enforcement
record indicates that they had been a little used
measure; there were only 58 fair wages arbitration
cases heard between 1946 and 1975, although the
number increased significantly in the subsequent
years of incomes policy.   This sort of evidence
may not, however, provide a sufficient basis for
fully assessing their worth if their major influence
has been through example, moral suasion and the
harnessing of self interest in favour of compliance.
Nevertheless, the most detailed empirical study of
the workings and impact of this resolution found
little support for the type of strong, positive
conclusion suggested above.   Specifically in

relation to union recognition it concluded that 'in the eyes of the Industrial Court and Government departments, anti-union attitudes and behaviour, even when openly exhibited, did not render employers in breach of the Fair Wages Resolution. In terms of the protection of trade union rights, Clause 4 has been useless'.(22) More generally, the resolution was seen to be influential only in the negative sense that:(23)

> By its very presence it forced the trade union movement to rely on its own strength and organisation to attain its objectives. Not being able to rely on the Fair Wages Resolution and in the knowledge that they would not receive any other help in this area, the trade unions took the hard road to self-reliant collective bargaining, independent of any legal protection or privilege through Government intervention. It is this which may be said to be the 'contribution' of the Fair Wages Resolution to collective bargaining and industrial relations in the United Kingdom.

In short, according to this particular study, the Fair Wages Resolution was unsuccessful as a means of transferring Government best practice (in the sense of active union encouragement) to the private sector. The reason typically given for this failure being the absence of administrative resources to monitor seriously its operation and consequently the invocation of few penalties or sanctions against offenders. On this view, the decision to repeal the resolution would appear to be of more symbolic than substantive importance. Moreover, it is worth noting that the Association of Metropolitan Authorities has advised its member authorities to continue to include fair wages clauses in their contract terms. This is still lawful, although Sections 12 and 13 of the Employment Act 1982 do render tender lists of only unionised firms unlawful.

The Decertification at GCHQ

The events leading up to the union decertification at GCHQ have been spelt out in some detail in a recent article,(24) so that only the briefest outline will be provided here. The first point to note is that traditionally employees at GCHQ were treated no differently from the rest of the civil service, at least in the sense of being encouraged to join trade unions. Employees at GCHQ were involved in the civil service wide pay dispute of 1979 and in subsequent cases of industrial action which led to government claims of the threat posed to national security by such action. Informal, unofficial talks between government and union representatives at GCHQ in 1980 produced little tangible outcome, but matters were brought to a head by the 'Prime Affair'; this involved a member of staff at GCHQ being jailed in 1982 after being found guilty of passing secret information to the Soviet Union. This led to the proposal for the introduction and use of lie detector machines (polygraphs) at GCHQ, a proposal that was opposed by the staff and union concerned. The apparent stalemate over the introduction of lie detectors was broken by the Government's announcement (with no prior staff consultation) that from 1st March 1984 GCHQ staff would no longer be permitted to be members of a trade union or have recourse to industrial tribunals. They could only belong in the future to an approved departmental staff association. The choices offered to the staff were resign union membership, receive £1,000 compensation and continue working at GCHQ, or apply for a transfer elsewhere in the civil service.

Discussions about a no-strike agreement, as a substitute for union decertification, came to nothing and by 1st March it was apparent that the vast majority of GCHQ's 8,000 staff had accepted the new working arrangements. There were protest stoppages in the public sector (involving some 120,000 working days lost in the quarter ending March 1984), the TUC temporarily withdrew from the National Economic Development Council, and the Government's action was challenged in the courts; the Law Lords unanimously dismissed the union's appeal, although the Council of Civil Service Unions are to take the case to the European Court of Human Rights. Nearly a year after the original prohibition, 58% of respondents in an employee ballot at GCHQ (with a 66% turnout rate) voted in favour of a new staff association, the Government Communications Staff Federation, whose constitution prohibits all forms of industrial action.

The important question raised by the union decertification at GCHQ is whether it was a one-off, special case, as opposed to raising the possibility of '... further incursions into the union rights of workers in defence-related and other sensitive

areas of employment, and that the removal of union
representation might encourage more employers in
the private sector to withdraw union recognition'.
(25)   The Government initiative at GCHQ is
certainly consistent with the nature of other actual
and contemplated changes in the larger context of
public sector industrial relations.   One thinks
here of the employment reductions already observed,
the attempts to reduce the priority attached to
comparability as a wage criterion (witness the
report of the Megaw Committee of Inquiry into the
civil service), and the use of pay assumptions in
cash limits as a public sector specific incomes
policy.   One indication of the degree of success
of the latter policy is provided by the following
figures (which were extracted from the relevant
issues of the New Earnings Survey) showing the
percentage increase in average gross weekly earnings for the period 1979/1980 to 1983/1984:

Year	Public Sector	Private Sector
1979-1980	25.6 (men)	20.6 (men)
	26.6 (women)	22.5 (women)
1980-1981	13.9 (men)	12.0 (men)
	18.0 (women)	14.5 (women)
1981-1982	8.4 (men)	10.9 (men)
	6.3 (women)	10.3 (women)
1982-1983	7.5 (men)	8.6 (men)
	9.6 (women)	9.7 (women)
1983-1984	6.3 (men)	9.8 (men)
	4.8 (women)	9.2 (women)

     The above indicates that wage increases in the
public sector generally exceeded those in the
private sector in 1979-1980 and 1980-1981 (the
Clegg Comparability Commission being an obvious
influence here), whilst the opposite tendency was
apparent in the years from 1981/1982.   Furthermore,
a comparison of the settlements of individual
negotiating groups in the public sector with the
relevant pay assumptions in the cash limits (14%
in 1980-1981, 6% in 1981-1982, 4% in 1982-1983,
3.5% in 1983-1984 and 3% in 1984-1985) indicates
that the former generally exceeded the latter in
any year, although the Government could clearly
claim some success in bringing down settlement
levels in consecutive years.   Focusing specifically
on the level of union organisation, one should
also note the following:

(i)   British Gas, British Telecom, the Post
Office and all water authorities (with British
Rail likely to follow) have all terminated their
closed shop agreements;
(ii)   the latest edition of the civil service
staff handbook no longer encourages employees to
join a union; it merely says they can join;
(iii)   the Government has expressed the desire to
bring the expenditure on lay union representatives
in the civil service (estimated at 0.3% of the
salary bill) under tighter control and to monitor
it continually.   To this end the national
facilities agreement has been revised with
individual departments renegotiating their own
agreements;
(iv)   the Cassells report on personnel management
in the civil service has recommended that relatively
more authority be accorded to individual departments
and to line managers;
(v)   the Government has accorded increased
representation and status to 'non-militant'
organisations on various public sector negotiating
bodies,(as in the case of the Professional
Association of Teachers receiving a seat on the
Burnham committee.)
     It is the continuation, and possible enhance-
ment, of moves along these lines that seems more
likely than further decertification moves in the
public sector.   In addition the Government is
known to favour the introduction of no-strike
arrangements in the public sector.   The calls for
the introduction of such agreements have frequently
followed major public sector disputes, such as
that of the firemen's strike of 1977 (see The
Economist, 19th November 1977).   More recently,
a report by the Centre for Policy Studies called
for such restrictions to be introduced for the
health service, the fire service, gas, electricity,
water, and local authority workers responsible for
burials and cremation.(26)   The arguments typically
presented in favour of such restrictions include
reference to the government as sovereign employer,
the belief that public sector unions are in a
relatively strong bargaining position and that
strikes in the public sector are especially high
cost ones to any third parties indirectly involved;
the latter is the most intuitively appealing one,
although at present it is more an a priori belief
than an established, empirical fact.   To date
there has been little tangible outcome from the

discussions on this subject, presumably as a consequence of disagreements over the definition or scope
of 'essential services' in the public sector and
over the desirability of institutionalising
compulsory arbitration arrangements in return for
removing the right to strike.

Decertification Tendencies in General

In Chapter 3 we outlined an argument to the effect
that statutory recognition provisions may entail
awkward legislative quid pro quos for any trade
union movement, the most obvious of these taking
the form of decertification procedures.   The two
sets of statutory recognition provisions that have
operated in Great Britain have in fact contained
decertification procedures.   Under the 1971 Act
some 35 applications were made (by April 1974) for
the withdrawal of recognition, with about half of
these involving members of the EETPU or ASTMS.
These latter figures suggested that this particular
provision was used in a quite different way to that
envisaged by those framing the legislation;(27)
that is, rather than individuals in a bargaining
unit questioning the representativeness of their
bargaining agent (with a view to moving to non-
union status) it was used by these two TUC affiliated unions as a substitute for their inability to
initiate a recognition claim.   In the case of
Sections 11-16 of the Employment Protection Act 1975
the ACAS Annual Report of 1980 indicated that some
20% of employers covered by an ACAS recommendation
had sought to have this revoked through the terms
of Section 13.(28)   In practice, however, none of
these applications succeeded in obtaining a
revocation;   the ACAS report indicated that the
legislation had failed to provide any formal
criteria to assist their decision making on this
matter.
     As indicated earlier, it is obviously an
extremely difficult task to see whether the union
decertification at GCHQ has stimulated or encouraged
similar management action in the private sector.
Indeed it is not even easy to assess the general
extent of such activity, regardless of its particular source or motivation.   However, the ACAS
Annual Report for 1984 did state that the service
'was involved in, or aware of, a number of
situations where employers sought to modify or
withdraw from existing recognition agreements'.(29)
As regards the modification of procedural agreements
we have already mentioned the cases of management's

desired (and actual) removal of the unilateral
right to arbitration in the banks and in the public
sector.   Company divestments is arguably an area
of corporate activity which could well be associated with a resulting above average opportunity
for union decertification.   Although current
estimates of the extent of divestment activity are
not readily available, some figures for the years
1969-1978 indicate that divested subsidiaries
accounted for more than 20% of the total number of
companies acquired in every year since 1970.(30)
The question of union decertification was, in fact,
explicitly examined in a recent study of some 111
management buy-outs.(31)   The basic finding was
that in less than 10% of cases (N = 9) had unions
ceased to be recognised in the post buy-out situation, and that in only one case had this been the
result of a deliberate choice or decision by management;   the remainder were a function of 'inertia',
rather than choice.   A more conventional recent
merger involving NABISCO taking over Huntley and
Palmer foods (in 1982) led to a subsequent re-
organisation of the management structure, with
ASTMS losing recognition;   more interestingly (in
view of the basic argument of Chapter 1), no trade
union is to be newly recognised (or derecognised)
for purposes of collective bargaining without
consultation with head office at Reading.(32)
        One well publicised attempt at decertification
occurred in ICI.   In 1976 ICI had recognised the
Association of Managerial and Professional Staff
(AMPS) as the bargaining agent for its 9,000 managerial and professional staff.   However, falling
membership and financial difficulties led AMPS to
merge with the EETPU in 1983, a decision which was
followed by ICI's announcement (in January 1984)
that it was giving six months notice of its
intention to terminate its recognition agreement
with AMPS.   The announcement was justified on the
grounds of the changed character of AMPS (following
its merger), and the desire of the company to deal
with managerial and professional staff on a more
individual basis.   The company's basic proposal
was that AMPS should have only consultation, as
opposed to negotiating, rights for this category of
staff.   Following expressions of individual
employee opposition, ICI withdrew (in mid-1984) its
notice of termination, with the 1976 agreement
remaining in force pending further talks between
the company and AMPS.   The real interest in the

ICI case would seem to lie in the fact that a large
well known company in the UK did not, even in the
absence of statutory provisions, consider decertification to be outwith the bounds of 'acceptable'
industrial relations practice at the present time.
However, discussions with organisations such as
IDS do not lead us to believe that the current
extent of decertification activity should be a
priority concern of the trade union movement.   This
seems consistent with the view put forward in
Chapter 1, namely that the actual lapsing or
decertification of unionised arrangements is unlikely to figure in the 'early stages' of any
adverse management reaction to unionisation.

Conclusions
The evidence presented in this chapter leads us to
conclude that there is relatively little likelihood
of a significant further increase in union density
in the public sector.   This prediction reflects
not only the nature of present Government attitudes
and actions towards trade unions, but also more
long standing factors, such as the relatively high
level of union density already achieved there.
Accordingly, if there is a significant increase
in overall union density in the UK throughout the
remainder of this decade (which is itself unlikely),
the public sector is unlikely to figure prominently
in it.
      What is the likelihood that the present Govern-
ment will have acted as an opinion leader, with its
attitudes and actions towards trade unions having
stimulated a similar response in the private sector?
One answer to this question might be to point to
the relative absence of historical evidence indicating that the Government as an employer has significantly influenced private sector practice;   recall,
in particular, the discussion of the Fair Wages
Resolution.   This apparently limited impact may be
due to the fact that public sector experience does
not generalise to the private sector, or at least
private sector employers do not believe that it
does.   Alternatively, it may be due to the
essential absence of institutional mechanisms for
affecting the transfer of practices across to the
private sector.   Whatever the relative importance
of these two factors, the fact that the good
employer example has not spread widely might lead
some commentators to believe the converse, i.e.
that the 'bad example' will not spread widely.

Such a view does, however, risk ignoring the fact that this role model provided by the present Government is closely linked (in timing terms) with measures that enhance the potential ability of private sector management to move in the desired direction. The particular measures that we have in mind here are contained in the Government's programme of industrial relations legislation, one aspect of which is considered in the next chapter.

NOTES

1. Alan Arthurs, "Industrial Relations in the Civil Service: Beyond GCHQ", Industrial Relations Journal, Vol.16, No.2, Summer 1985, p.29.

2. B. Hepple, "Labour Law and Public Employees in Britain", in W. Wedderburn and W.T. Murphy (eds), Labour Law and the Community, Institute of Advanced Legal Studies, University of London, 1982, pp.67–83.

3. Hepple in Wedderburn and Murphy (eds) op.cit., p.78.

4. Report of the Royal Commission on the Civil Service, 1953–1955, Cmnd 9613, para 146, p.39.

5. Staff Relations in the Civil Service, HMSO, London, 1949, p.3.

6. See, for example, David Lockwood, The Black Coated Worker, Allen and Unwin, London, 1958.

7. Ken Prandy, "Professional Organisations in Great Britain", Industrial Relations, Vol.5, October 1965, p.73.

8. R.M. Blackburn, Union Character and Social Class, Batsford, London, 1967.

9. I.G. Richardson, "Employment in the Public and Private Sectors, 1978 to 1984", Economic Trends, No. 377, March 1985, p.93.

10. Economic Progress Report No. 168, HM Treasury, June 1984, p.3.

11. Civil Service Statistics 1984, HM Treasury, July 1984, p.8.

12. D. Fatchett and S. Ogden, "Public Expenditure Cuts and Job Loss: A Union Response", Journal of Management Studies, Vol.21, 1984, pp.207–227.

13. Cited in David Metcalf, "On the Measurement of Employment and Unemployment", National Institute Economic Review, No.109, August 1984, p.66.

14. John Lloyd, Financial Times, 27th June 1985.

15.   David Heald, Public Expenditure, Martin
Robertson, London, 1983, p.298.

16.   Heald, op.cit. p.299

17.   Heald, ibid., p.229.

18.   J.W. Leopold and P.B. Beaumont, "Arbitration Arrangements in the Public Sector in Britain", The Arbitration Journal, Vol.38, No.2, June 1983, p.57.

19.   J. Sherman, "Waiting for the Big Bite", Health and Social Services Journal, 27th June 1985, p.206.

20.   Brian Bercusson, Fair Wages Resolution, Mansell, London, 1978, p.101.

21.   O. Kahn-Freund, "Legislation Through Adjudication: The Legal Aspect of Fair Wages Clauses and Recognised Conditions", Modern Law Review, Vol.11, 1948, p.274.

22.   Bercusson, op.cit., p.345.

23.   Bercusson, ibid., p.107.

24.   Arthurs, Loc.cit.

25.   Arthurs, ibid., p.29.

26.   Cited in John Lover, "The Anti-Strike Hit List", Management Today, January 1985, p.75.

27.   Brian Weekes et al, Industrial Relations and the Limits of the Law, Blackwell, Oxford, 1975, pp. 147-150.

28.   ACAS Annual Report 1980, HMSO, London, 1981, p.91.

29.   ACAS Annual Report 1984, HMSO, London, 1985, p.22.

30.   Brian Chiplin and Mike Wright, "Divestment and Structural Change in UK Industry", National Westminster Bank Quarterly Review, February 1980, p.43.

31.   Mike Wright and John Coyne, Management Buy Outs, Croom Helm, London, 1985, pp.116-121.

32.   Industrial Relations Review and Report, No.351, September 1985.

Chapter Seven

DEALING WITH 'FREE RIDERS'

In the previous chapter we considered the government's role of public sector employer (and paymaster) as a possible influence working to reduce the overall level of union density in the UK.   The other major Government role considered now is its legislative one; both Chapter 3 (repeal of the statutory recognition provisions) and Chapter 5 (encouragement of the small firm sector) have, of course, touched on this matter.   Given the particular focus of this book, the importance of the legislative role is that it can, at any point in time, potentially increase (or decrease) the range of options or means open to a management wishing to operate on a non-union basis or with little increase in the union density of its partially unionised workforce.

The broad ranging programme of industrial relations legislation of the present Government seeks to constrain both the behavioural (e.g. strike) and institutional (e.g. closed shop) manifestations of 'union power', being based on a number of major (if not well established) assumptions such as the belief that a democratic union is a relatively strike-free union.   The major provisions of the Employment Acts of 1980 and 1982 and the Trade Union Act of 1984 have been summarised as follows:(1)

(i)   removal of legal immunities for picketing (other than by employees at their place of work) and for secondary industrial action;
(ii)   introduction and strengthening of the rights of employees dismissed for refusing to join closed shops;

172

(iii)   institution of secret ballots to approve new closed shops and to confirm previous closed shops; dismissal on membership grounds will only be 'fair' if the closed shop is approved by a ballot held within the preceding five years;

(iv)   lengthening the period of employment before complaints of unfair dismissal can be made from six to twelve months, and to two years for firms with less than 20 employees;

(v)   removal of legal immunities from civil actions so as to make trade unions subject to injunctions and damages when they are responsible for unlawful industrial action;

(vi)   removal of legal immunities from civil actions in any industrial action which has not been agreed in advance by a secret ballot of the membership;

(vii)   executive committees of trade unions to be elected by secret ballot at least every five years.

It has been argued that the nature of changes in industrial relations legislation can be understood as a response to major changes in (i) the political access of interest groups, and (ii) the ideology towards property rights (conversely towards organised labour) in the larger society.(2) If one wished to utilise this framework to try and account for the content of the current Government's programme of industrial relations legislation one could certainly instance the 'freeze-out' of the TUC in the consultative process, the apparent increased influence of the Institute of Directors (relative to the CBI) with their stress on the primacy of the individual-organisation relationship, and a reaction to the Gallup Polls of the late 1970s reporting a public perception of 'excessive' trade union power in the UK. An alternative view might simply be that from the early '70s there has been a political cycle in the UK whereby a new government which is either pro-union or pro-employer seeks to repeal the legislation (and associated administrative arrangements and procedures) of its predecessor. This latter view might occasion some comfort to anyone believing that the present forces working against the maintenance of overall union density in the UK are the relatively short term ones of economic recession and the anti-union legislation of the present Government.

In the previous chapters we largely proceeded from the basis of a close relationship between union recognition and union density, with its obvious implication that the latter can be raised through the achievement of recognition for new bargaining units.   An alternative means of increasing union density, particularly in the UK, (as compared with the United States) is to seek to reduce the gap between collective bargaining cover- age (CBC) and union density (UD).   A major means to this end has been through the establishment of closed shop arrangements, the future of which has been called into question by the legislation of the present Government;   for this reason we focus here on this particular aspect of the Government's legislation.   This possibility may necessitate the unions paying increased attention to other possible means of reducing this gap.   Moreover, as we hope to show, the sizeable difference between collective bargaining coverage and union density in the UK is not simply due to the traditional free rider problem of individuals in a recognised bargaining unit not belonging to unions.   In view of this fact we begin this chapter with a comparison of the size difference between CBC and UD in the United States and the UK.

The Size Difference Between CBC and UD

In the United States union relative wage studies have tended to use the terms (and measures) collective bargaining coverage and union density almost interchangeably.   This practice does not appear to constitute too great a distortion of reality in view of the following figures (for the private sector):(3)

CBC	UD
(1968-72)	(1973-75)
29.8%	23.7%

In the aggregate it appears that CBC exceeds UD by about 6 percentage points, although consider- able inter-industry variation in the extent of the difference was apparent.   One of the major reasons given for this difference was the absence of union security clauses in a number of collective agreements;   in 1975 some 33% of major contracts (covering 1,000 workers or more) did not contain such clauses.(4)   The union shop (or post entry closed shop in British terminology) is the most common union security clause in the United States,

although there are some indications that the extent
of its coverage has declined in recent years.
Certainly, Hanson, Jackson and Miller report that
the proportion of workers covered by union shop
provisions fell from over 75% in 1972 to around 66%
in 1976.(5)   This sort of decline could be the
result of union shop de-authorisation elections.
These elections have certainly increased in recent
years, with approximately 6 out of every 10 of them
resulting in the de-authorisation of the union shop
(particularly in small sized bargaining units);
the absolute numbers involved (e.g. 140 elections
in 1978), however, are small.(6)   A much more
potent influence would appear to be the existence
of 'right to work' legislation (which prohibits
union security clauses) in some 20 states.   These
are overwhelmingly the 'sun-belt' states of the
southern and western parts of the USA, which are
very much the employment growth areas of the
country;   for example, manufacturing employment in
the south-east and south-west grew by 18% and 40%
respectively between 1966 and 1977, whereas it
fell by some 12% in New England.   The level of
union density in all of these right to work states
was below the all-state average (approximately 24%)
in the late 1970s, with only Nevada being ranked
in the first 25 states according to union density.
There has in fact been a long standing debate over
the significance of the right to legislation, with
earlier studies tending to suggest that it was of
more symbolic, than substantive, importance.
However, the most recent study estimates that the
difference between CBC and UD in these particular
states is significantly greater than that elsewhere.
(7)
        In Chapters 3 and 4 we made some estimates of
the respective contributions of statutory recognition and voluntary conciliation provisions to the
growth of total union membership in the years
1976-1980.   These estimates took explicit account
of the difference between CBC and UD by comparing
Price and Bain's figures for the latter with some
estimates for CBC that were contained in the New
Earnings Survey for 1973 and 1978.   The basic
figures in this regard were as follows:

	1973	1978
CBC	71.8%	68.8%
UD	49.3%	54.2%

The fall in CBC between these years, at a time
when UD was clearly increasing, was something of a
surprise, perhaps being best explained by the
respondents to the 1978 survey being influenced by
an extended period of incomes policy.(8)   The
above figures do make it difficult to avoid the
conclusion that the gap between CBC and UD in the
UK is rather greater than that in the United States;
in the 1960s some rough estimates by individuals,
such as Flanders, even suggested a difference as
great as some 35 percentage points.(9)

Bargaining Structure and the Capacity to Pattern Follow

The relatively large difference between CBC and UD
in the UK has both an inter-organisational and an
intra-organisational component to it, although the
relative importance of them is difficult to
establish at the present time.   The inter-organisational component derives from the traditional
multi-employer, industry level bargaining structure
of the UK which has allowed non-union establishments
to set their terms and conditions of employment by
reference to the relevant industry agreement.
These 'pattern followers' are likely to be mainly
small, non-federated employers, particularly in
relatively labour intensive industries;(10)   the
presence of shift work arrangements and payment by
results schemes would also appear to stimulate such
activity.   This inter-organisational source of the
difference between CBC and UD would appear to be
of lesser significance in recent years, given the
substantial movement towards single employer
bargaining arrangements at the plant, and to a
lesser extent the company, level;   this is, of
course, only a private sector phenomenon as
industry level bargaining arrangements still
dominate the public sector (the substantial growth
of payment by results schemes in local government
and the NHS in the 1970s is, of course, acknowledged
here).   At the present time any large scale survey
in the UK will typically reveal that upwards of
75% of the respondent establishments report their
most important level of wage bargaining as a single
employer one.   There are still, however, some
important inter-industry differences in this regard,
with multi-employer, industry level wage bargaining
remaining important in industries characterised by
small firm size, spatial concentration and competitive product markets.   The industries where

industry wage agreements still constitute 'floors'
(rather than 'safety nets') and thus permit
meaningful pattern following by non-union establishments are suggested by the figures set out in Table
7.1.

Table 7.1:   The Relative Importance of Multi-
             employer, Industry Level Bargaining,
             Manufacturing Sector, 1977-1978

Industry	Multi-employer as % of single plus multi-employer bargaining level
Food	25
Coal products	0
Chemicals	20
Metal manufacture	15
Mechanical engineering	6
Instrument engineering	7
Electrical engineering	6
Shipbuilding	9
Vehicles	5
Metal goods	10
Textiles	55
Leather	43
Clothing	51
Bricks	36
Timber	43
Paper	81
Other manufacture	18
Total	25

Source: D.R. Deaton and P.B. Beaumont, 'The
          Determinants of Bargaining Structure:
          Some Large Scale Survey Evidence for
          Britain', British Journal of Industrial
          Relations, Vol.XVIII, No. 2, July 1980,
          p.205.

The industries which stand out above are
obviously printing, textiles, leather and clothing,
indicating that the capacity to pattern follow
still appears to remain in its traditional stronghold industries;   recent discussions with trade
union officers in Glasgow suggested that this
particular practice is actually on the increase

outside manufacturing, namely in the construction
industry.

Free Riding and the Closed Shop

The intra-organisational component of the difference
between CBC and UD is the one traditionally discussed in the literature, namely that due to
individuals in a recognised bargaining unit not
being members of the union or bargaining agent.
To the unions such an individual is analagous to
the consumer of a public good in that such a person
receives, but does not pay for, the benefits of an
indivisible service; hence the term 'free rider'.
Individual unions in the UK have periodically drawn
attention to this phenomenon, typically along the
following lines:(11)

> It will ... be a source of annoyance to
> reasonable people that the five thousand
> non-members of the Association who are
> serving as university teachers, adminis-
> trators, librarians and research staff,
> will pocket these increases and back-pay
> without contributing to them. One hears
> a great deal about those who on
> conscientious grounds will not join their
> fellows in an organisation responsible
> for negotiations on conditions of employ-
> ment. One hears very little about a lack
> of conscience on the part of those who
> take without contributing.

This particular attempt at moral suasion is of
interest in using the term 'reasonable' in that
John R. Commons' whole argument that individual
freedom was only something that could be achieved
through a collective adherence to duties that
define and protect individual rights for everyone
was underpinned by the concept of a reasonable
individual.(12) The contrasting view of Olson
takes as its starting point the notion of a rational
individual, arguing that the influence of trust,
friendship, social pressure or altruistic concern
for the welfare of the group as a whole is relatively slight on an individual being asked to contribute
to collective goods in larger group settings.(13)
To Olson, the closed shop is a necessary institutional response to this particular phenomenon; it
goes without saying that not all industrial
relations commentators would accept the validity
of the public good argument in relation to unions.

Dealing with 'Free Riders'

     There have been a number of recent general and
specialist surveys on the extent of closed shop
arrangements in Britain, with all of them indicating
that coverage has increased significantly from the
early 1960s.   The 1980 workplace industrial
relations survey, for example, reported that some
27 per cent of employees at the surveyed establishments were covered by a closed shop;(14)   the
latter figure was compared to McCarthy's estimate
of 16 per cent of employees (employed and unemployed) covered by such arrangements in 1962.   Further
analysis revealed that the closed shop was princip-
ally a manual worker phenomenon (44 per cent of
manuals covered compared to 9 per cent of non-
manuals) and that the incidence of closed shops
was particularly associated with nationalised
industries, large establishment size, and larger
organisation size.   Moreover, the vast majority
of the growth in closed shops has taken the form
of post-entry arrangements.   The position by
individual industry, at least as revealed by the
Dunn and Gennard study, is set out below in Table
7.2.
     This particular study noted that the individual
industries where the closed shop has spread most
rapidly included food,drink and tobacco, clothing
and footwear, public utilities,and transport and
communications.
     In considering the prospects for an extension
of closed shop arrangements in the 1980s, Dunn and
Gennard highlighted a number of potential constraining factors.(15)   These included the disproportionate concentration of employment declines in the
manufacturing industries traditionally associated
with the closed shop, the relative growth of private
services employment where such arrangements are
little established (due to limited union recognition
and management opposition), and the relevant
provisions of the Employment Acts 1980 and 1982.
Among the most relevant provisions here are the
following:

(i)   Where there is a union membership agreement it will be unfair to dismiss on grounds of
non-membership of a union where:
          (a)   the employee objects to membership
          on grounds of conscience or other deeply
          held genuine personal conviction to being a
          member of any trade union whatsoever or of
          a particular trade union;

Table 7.2: The Closed Shop Pattern by Industry, 1978

Industry	% of workers covered by survey in closed shops	Minimum % of total workforce in closed shops
Agriculture	1	1
Mining	87	87
Food, drink & tobacco	53	38
Coal and petroleum	67	55
Chemicals	42	32
Metal manufacture	62	50
Mechanical engineering	52	45
Instrument engineering	13	10
Electrical engineering	35	30
Shipbuilding	68	57
Vehicles	57	48
Metal goods	39	33
Textiles	30	21
Leather	15	14
Clothing	28	23
Bricks	46	33
Timber	39	29
Paper	79	66
Other manufacturing	50	41
Construction	8	7
Gas	81	80
Transport	69	56
Distributive	18	15
Insurance	6	5
Professional services	4	3
Miscellaneous services	6	6
Public administration	17	14
TOTAL	27.6	23.3

Source: Stephen Dunn and John Gennard, The Closed Shop in British Industry, Macmillan, London, 1984, p.16.

> (b) the employee was working before the
> union membership agreement came into effect
> and at no time had been a member of that
> trade union;
> (c) a closed shop coming into effect after
> the 1980 Act became operative is not
> approved in a secret ballot by at least 80
> per cent of employees entitled to vote
> having been given a reasonable opportunity
> of doing so;
> (d) a closed shop coming into effect after
> the Act became operative has been approved
> by 80 per cent of employees but an existing
> employee has not been a member of a specified
> union since the date of the ballot.

(ii)   As from 1 November 1984 a closed shop
dismissal for non-membership will be unfair if the
closed shop agreement has not been approved by
ballot within the five years prior to the dismissal.
The ballot (except for the first ballot of a new
agreement) requires approval by 80 per cent of those
entitled to vote or 85 per cent of those voting.
(iii)   Any term in a commercial contract is void if
it requires the contractor to operate a closed
shop.
(iv)   Industrial action aimed at imposing this
practice is unlawful.

A code of practice on closed shop agreements
and arrangements has also been issued, the provisions of which have been described as follows:(16)

> This part contains the first group of forty or
> more obstacles, conditions or exceptions
> intended to induce employers to prevaricate.
> The guidance is essentially confined to
> suggestions limiting the circumstances in
> which employers should agree to and unions
> should press for closed shops ... The anti-
> closed shop tone is equally strong in the
> Code's guidance on the scope and content of
> closed shop agreements ... Perhaps the most
> provocative and dubious part of the Code is
> suggested provision for periodic review of
> existing closed shops and a procedure for
> their termination.

In view of the latter observation it is worth
indicating the review provisions of the Code:

(i)   Reviews of agreements should take place every few years and more frequently if changes of the following types occur:
> (a)   where there is evidence that the support of the employees for a closed shop has declined;
> (b)   where there has been a change in the parties to an agreement;
> (c)   where there is evidence that the agreement, or parts of it, are not working satisfactorily;
> (d)   where there is a change in the law affecting the closed shop.

(ii)   If following this review the parties agree that the agreement should continue, they should ensure that it has the continued support of the employees concerned.   A secret ballot should be held if one has not taken place previously or for some considerable time.

(iii)   No new pre-entry closed shop agreements should be made and the continuation of existing pre-entry closed shops should be carefully reviewed.

Although Dunn and Gennard concluded that 'by 1980 compulsory unionism had come to exist in most areas where conditions were conducive to it' (17) they were understandably reluctant to predict (because of the uncertainty of management attitudes) whether the provisions of the 1980 and 1982 Acts would lead to the dismantling or lapsing of existing closed shop arrangements.   Similarly, Brown and Sisson offer little more than the observation that 'specific items of legislation, such as those providing opportunities to challenge closed shops, would probably play a lesser part in weakening collective bargaining than the more diffuse symbolic impact of the withdrawal of explicit government support'.(18)   On this matter of government support it is worth recalling the instances (noted in the previous chapter) of public sector management challenging the continuation of closed shop arrangements;   in this sense the government role may be more than a symbolic one. At the TUC Wembley conference of 1982 the general council observed that:(19)

> It would be dangerous for those unions with 100 per cent trade union membership agreements and arrangements to assume that there would be any significant advantage to them in participating in ballots held under a new Act about the continuation of these

arrangements. If ballots are held, a situation in which there are no problems would at
least be altered in such a way as to saddle
unions - and employers - with substantial
regular electioneering and upheaval. At
worst, any differences between sections of the
workforce about, for example, a pay agreement, would be intensified as a result of a
ballot on union membership: the result could
be internal strife, the undermining of
established negotiating rights and, in multi-
union establishments, inter-union difficulties.
Even where a ballot achieved the necessary
majority there are still substantial legal
bolt-holes in the 1980 Act through which
dismissed non-unionists can slip and win a
legal case and obtain compensation from an
employer or union or both.

The extent to which this recommendation has
been followed is not completely clear. The ACAS
Annual Report for 1984 did, however, note some 80
instances of closed shop ballots, with some 14 per
cent of these (N = 11) failing to achieve the
necessary levels of employee support.(20) The
survey by Edwards, which was referred to in Chapter
1, found no instances of the removal of closed
shops, although the fieldwork was conducted prior
to the balloting arrangements of the 1982 Act coming
into force.(21) The answer to a parliamentary
question in April 1985 noted the 80 instances of
closed shop ballots (mostly covering small groups
of employees) referred to above, and then went on
to comment that 'in addition a number of major
employers have ended their closed shops or given
a commitment that no-one will be dismissed for non-
union membership'.(22) A recent article in
Personnel Management has usefully outlined the
options and associated implications of these
balloting provisions.(23)

If non-union pattern following remains in the
particular industries identified and the growth of
closed shops is checked (if not reversed) then what
can the unions do to try and reduce the size of the
CBC-UD gap in the UK? One possibility is to seek
an increase in the extent of check-off arrangements
as a 'lesser substitute' for the closed shop.
In the late 1970s the TUC reported that some 50
per cent of affiliated membership was covered by
the check-off compared to only some 20 per cent
a decade earlier.(24) More recently, the 1980

workplace industrial relations survey reported
that nearly 50 per cent of establishments with
manual employees operated the check-off, and that
this proportion rose to 75 per cent of all establishments that recognised manual unions.(25)   The
Daniel and Millward analysis tended to cast doubt
on any suggestion that closed shop and check-off
arrangements are causally linked, although the fact
that the check-off was associated with relatively
high union density for manuals would seem to limit
its general applicability for trying to reduce the
CBC-UD gap.

An Individual Advocacy and Assistance Role
In contemplating other possible ways of reducing
this gap it is important to recognise that the full
range of potential services provided by a union
does not comprise solely collective services.
Pencavel, for example, has suggested that one can
usefully distinguish between the collective
services, semi-collective services and private
services provided by trade unions.(26)   Accordingly
one possible way to try and reduce the extent of the
above gap would be for unions to increase the
relative provision of services in the latter
categories.   In this regard a recent AFL-CIO
document suggested that unions in the United States
could usefully give more thought to the possibility
of negotiating minimum guarantees as a floor for
individual bargaining as well as adopting more of
an advocacy role for individual employees.(27)
Indeed this document even went as far as suggesting
that consideration be given to the creation of new
categories of membership for employees not in
recognised bargaining units.   This was deemed to
be particularly important in view of the likelihood
of increased worker mobility enhancing the need for
a range of employment services covering matters
such as training, medical insurance, information on
job openings and career advice.   This particular
recommendation is certainly in accord with Handy's
view (which we noted in Chapter 1) that trade unions
in the UK should increasingly assume an advisory-
advocacy role for individual employees a la the
guild model.
     A number of older studies in Britain reported
that the proportion of union expenditure on 'welfare
benefits' had tended to fall through time, largely
as a result of a relatively full employment environment and the increased government provision of such
benefits.(28)   At the present time there appears

to be considerable inter-union variation in the
extent of provision of private services or welfare
benefits. A TUC survey of some 84 unions in the
early 1980s reported the following position:

Individual Benefit	Number of unions providing it
Unemployment	22
Sick/accident	44
Permanent incapacity	24
Superannuation	10
Death/funeral	61
Benevolent grants	41
Legal aid	69

The NALGO document from which these figures
were drawn went on to comment that '... at a time
when union membership is falling and competition
between unions correspondingly acute, there are
clearly recruitment advantages in offering attractive fringe benefits'.(29)   Their attraction value
in this regard might appear to be questionable
given, for example, Blackburn's finding that the
provision of cheap insurance policies by NUBE only
influenced two of his sample respondents to join.
(30)   However, the potential importance of such
private services is arguably more in relation to
the marginal (rather than average) individual in a
recognised bargaining unit who is contemplating
the question of whether to retain or relinquish
free rider status.   The importance of such
services may reach beyond the individual free rider
issue to situations where unions are seeking to
bring about mergers with staff associations.   The
desire of employees in Kodak to obtain access to
union legal services to assist in accident compensation claims was mentioned in Chapter 5, while the
present ASTMS attempt to bring about association
agreements in the finance sector (Chapter 4) is very
much premised on the likely appeal of legal and
research facilities to potential merger partners.
It is also possible that these private services
could be a factor in accounting for any observed
inter-union variation in the extent to which the
unemployed retain union membership.
    Those advocating that unions adopt an increased
advocacy and assistance role for individual employees are, of course, arguing for more than simply a
return to a friendly society function.   The
expectation or hope is that the range of private
services will be built up from this traditional

185

base; the specific examples cited in the AFL-CIO
document should be recalled here. In the UK one
such example is provided by the EETPU who have had
their own technical training centre in Kent since
1980 which provides courses on new technology,
robotics, etc. In addition, training is provided
through mobile units on employers' premises and at
regional union offices, the result being the EETPU
claim, in a recent brochure, that '... members
can acquire through their union the appropriate
skills to design, install, commission and maintain
modern plant and machinery'. This particular
feature of the EETPU was one of the reasons, given
in Morgan and Sayers study, for employers in the
electronics industry in South Wales tending to
prefer to deal with them rather than with other
unions. In keeping with the AFL-CIO proposal
noted earlier, one union officer has recently
pointed to the possible virtues of creating an
associate category of union membership for employees
in small, private service sector establishments in
the UK.(31) In return for a lesser subscription
rate the union would provide representational
services for such individuals before bodies such as
industrial tribunals, information/advice on basic
terms and conditions of employment and welfare
benefits. The former benefits would seem particularly attractive given (as we noted in Chapter 1)
that it is individuals from such establishments
that are disproportionately involved in unfair
dismissal applications before industrial tribunals,
and with no entitlement to legal aid; the absence
of legal representation has certainly been related
to a reduced likelihood of winning the claim.(32)
Furthermore, the growth of part-time, temporary
and self-employment in the service sector raises
a number of important questions about the nature
of the individual contract of employment,(33) upon
which an individual could be expected to welcome
union advice.

Conclusions

In comparison with the US, the lesser extent of
both single employer bargaining and union security
provisions has traditionally resulted in a quite
sizeable difference between collective bargaining
coverage and union density in the UK. The changes
in these two features of the system of industrial
relations in the '70s would have generally operated
in the direction of reducing this difference.

Although public sector management could be argued
to be trying to show the way, there is little sign,
as yet, that management has taken the opportunity
provided by the present Government's legislation
to try and remove existing closed shop arrangements;
this is not, as we argued in Chapter 1, a likely,
early stage manifestation of any management reaction
against unions in the UK.

However, as with new bargaining units, one
can anticipate increased management resistance to
attempts to negotiate new closed shop arrangements.
In view of this strong likelihood, the union
movement may have to consider alternative ways of
trying to bridge this gap, some of which may
involve increased attention being given to the
needs of individual employees both in and outside
recognised bargaining units.

NOTES

1.   Cited in Christopher Story, "The Labour
Cartels: Has Anything Really Changed?", National
Westminster Bank Quarterly Review, May 1985,
pp.64-65.
2.   Sanford Cohen, "An Analytical Framework
for Labor Relations Law", Industrial and Labor
Relations Review, Vol.14, April 1961, pp.350-362.
3.   Richard B. Freeman and James L. Medoff,
"New Estimates of Private Sector Unionism in the
United States", Industrial and Labor Relations
Review, Vol.32, No.2, January 1979, p.169.
4.   Freeman and Medoff, op.cit., p.171.
5.   Charles Hanson, Sheila Jackson and
Douglas Miller, The Closed Shop, Gower, Aldershot,
Hants, 1982, p.162.
6.   James B. Dworkin and Marian M. Extejt,
"The Union-Shop Deauthorisation Poll: A New Look
After 20 Years", Monthly Labor Review, November
1979, p.38.
7.   David Ellwood and Glenn Fine, Effect of
Right to Work Laws on Union Organising, National
Bureau of Economic Research Working Paper No.1116,
May 1983.
8.   M.B. Gregory and A.W.J. Thomson, "The
Coverage, Mark-Up, Bargaining Structure and Earn-
ings in Britain, 1973 and 1978", British Journal
of Industrial Relations, Vol.XIX, No.1, March 1981,
pp.27-28.
9.   Allan Flanders, Collective Bargaining,
Faber, London, 1967, p.13.

10.   P.B. Beaumont and M.B. Gregory, "The Role of Employers in Collective Bargaining in Britain", Industrial Relations Journal, Vol.11, No.5, November-December 1980, pp.46-52.

11.   See John Hughes and Harold Pollins (eds) Trade Unions in Great Britain, David Charles, Newton Abbot, 1973, pp.31-33.

12.   John R. Commons, The Economics of Collective Action, University of Wisconsin Press, Madison, Wis., 1950.

13.   Mancur Olson, The Logic of Collective Agreement, Harvard University Press, Cambridge, Mass., 1965.

14.   W.W. Daniel and Neil Millward, Workplace Industrial Relations in Britain, Heinemann, London, 1983, pp.60-62.

15.   Stephen Dunn and John Gennard, The Closed Shop in British Industry, Macmillan, London, 1985, pp.145-156.

16.   Roy Lewis and Bob Simpson, Striking a Balance?, Martin Robertson, Oxford, 1981, pp.94-95.

17.   Dunn and Gennard, op.cit., p.148.

18.   William Brown and Keith Sisson, "Current Trends and Future Possibilities", in M. Poole et al, Industrial Relations in the Future, Routledge and Kegan Paul, London, 1984, p.15.

19.   Report by the TUC General Council, Industrial Relations Legislation, April 1982, p.18.

20.   ACAS Annual Report 1984, HMSO, London, 1985, p.10.

21.   P.K. Edwards, "Managing Labour Relations Through the Recession", Employee Relations, Vol.7, No.2, 1985, p.4.

22.   Employment Gazette, April 1985, p.157.

23.   Cory Roberts, "Who Will Bite the Closed Shop Ballot?", Personnel Management, October 1984, pp.44-46.

24.   "The Check-Off System: A Review of Some Recent Agreements", Industrial Relations Review and Report, No.196, March 1979, pp.2-6.

25.   Daniel and Millward, op.cit., pp.75-76.

26.   John H. Pencavel, "The Demand for Union Services: An Exercise", Industrial and Labor Relations Review, Vol.24, No.2, January 1971, p.181.

27.   Cited in Industrial Relations Review and Report, No.343, May 1985.

28.   B.C. Roberts, Trade Union Government and Administration in Great Britain, Bell and Sons, London, 1956, Appendix 7, p.384.
29.   NALGO, Benefits of Union Membership, January 1985, p.2.
30.   R.M. Blackburn, Union Character and Social Class, Batsford, London, 1967, p.208.
31.   Larry Cairns, "Union Membership Recruitment - a New Approach", Scottish Trade Union Review, No.27, February-April 1985, pp.33-35.
32.   Linda Dickens, "Industrial Tribunals - The Peoples Courts", Employee Relations, Vol.7, No.1. 1985, p.30.
33.   Patricia Leighton, "Employment and Self-Employment: Some Problems of Law and Practice", Employment Gazette, May 1983, p.197-203.

Chapter Eight

CONCLUSIONS

In this final chapter we draw together the arguments of previous chapters, outline some future
research needs and suggest some possible changes
that may be of interest to anyone concerned with
the likelihood of a further fall in the level of
union density in the UK.

At the level of the individual organisation
it has been argued that the <u>motivation</u> to avoid
unions is a negative function of the degree to
which labour costs have been taken out of competition, while the <u>ability</u> to achieve this end is
negatively related to the current level of unionisation and positively related to the extent of
decentralised collective bargaining.(1)   If these
factors are aggregated to the level of a national
system of industrial relations then it would suggest
that, at any point in time, a future increase in
union density will be relatively difficult to
achieve in a system characterised by plant level
collective bargaining, substantial foreign competition, and a relatively low level of union density.
Two of these three factors are, of course, currently
present in the UK.   The movement towards a system
of single employer bargaining arrangements, predominantly at the plant level, has particularly
important potential implications for the future
level of union density in the UK.   Under such
arrangements, union relative wage effects are
likely to increase, while the frequency of strikes
is also alleged to rise,(2) the result being an
increased cost incentive for management to move
away from an acceptance of unionisation; this will
be particularly the case in a highly competitive
and integrated product market environment which
places great store on the necessity for organi-

sational flexibility.   And at the same time there
is relatively little capacity to extend recognition
arrangements through the medium of powerful and
influential employers associations;   a government's
incentive to try and act in this way is also reduced
by the limited capacity of a trade union federation
to ensure, as a quid pro quo, wage restraint among
its affiliated organisations.   These are some of
the factors that would appear to lie behind the
negative correlation between single employer bargaining structures and the level of union density
that is revealed in cross-country studies;(3)   the
positive correlation between single employer bargaining structures and statutory recognition provisions would also seem explicable in these terms.(4)

     As well as the extent of management opposition
to unions, one also needs to consider the nature
of such opposition, which will be determined by
both practical (cost) and legal considerations.
On the latter point it is interesting to note that
a recent article in the United States has suggested
unions could possibly successfully protest against
a unionised firm dealing with its employees in a
non-union forum (as occurs in 'double-breasted'
operations there) with the employee participation
structure (e.g. quality circles) likely to be
dissolved as a remedy.(5)   The material presented
in the previous chapters suggests that it is
possible to derive a checklist of factors likely
to hinder the extent of union density in any
national system of industrial relations.   These
factors, which shape both the extent and nature of
management opposition to unions, are set out in
Table 8.1.

     Although the 'idealised' list in the Table
does not perfectly approximate any national system
of industrial relations, its contents should help
make clear why the prospects for a future increase
in union density in the United States would appear
to be considerably less than those in the UK at the
present time.   It is essential to emphasise the
phrase 'at the present time' because it is arguable,
some would say likely, that the extent and nature
of management opposition to unions will be positively related to the extent of prior union decline;
in this regard recall that union density in the UK
only peaked some 6 years ago, whereas in the United
States union density has been declining in the
private sector for more than 2 decades.   In other
words, the US and the UK are likely to be at quite
different stages in a process of management

Table 8.1:   A Checklist of Factors Likely to Limit
             the Extent of Union Density

1.   An Economic system characterised by:

    (i)   a sustained period of high unemployment
             /low inflation;
    (ii)   substantial foreign competition;
    (iii)   a relatively sizeable and growing
             private services sector;
    (iv)   a relatively high proportion of single,
             independent establishments;
    (v)   a sizeable (in land mass terms) economy
             with a geographically dispersed pattern
             of employment;

2.   A Political system characterised by:

    (i)   a party that is not well disposed
             towards unions being in office during
             a period of time in which fundamental
             (i.e. non-incremental) changes in the
             economic environment are occurring;
    (ii)   the existence of state level legis-
             lation which institutionalises area
             or regional opposition to unions;

3.   An Industrial Relations system characterised
     by:

    (i)   plant level collective bargaining;
    (ii)   union density falling over an
             extended period of time;
    (iii)   relatively long standing legislation
             providing rights for individual
             employees, over and above trade union
             membership status;
    (iv)   relatively long standing legislation
             providing for the decertification of
             unionised structures;
    (v)   the relative absence of national,
             integrating legislation on job security
             matters, providing rights for
             individual employees and unions as
             institutions.

Conclusions

opposition to unions, so that one is not comparing
like with like.   The evidence presented here
suggests that in the UK this early stage opposition
is certainly reflected in (i) attempts to limit
recognition being obtained for uncovered bargaining
units in partially unionised establishments, and
(ii) an increase in the number of non-union establishments, while other survey work indicates that
some attempt is being made to (iii) limit the
number, and influence, of shop stewards which may,
in turn, suggest (iv) a reduction in the scope or
range of bargaining.   The available evidence for
the UK certainly does not indicate that management
has reached the stage of the US where unionised
structures are being formally lapsed or decertified, or undermined through the opening of non-
union plants in individual organisations.   For the
reasons given (see Table 8.1) this would seem a
more difficult stage for UK management to ever
reach.   However, before one could be fully con-
fident of such a conclusion there is clearly a good
deal of further research that is necessary.   The
next section outlines some of the research needs
in this regard.

Future Research Needs
Most of the areas or subjects requiring further
research have been indicated in previous chapters
so that only the briefest outline will be provided
here.   On the basis of what has gone before, we
would highlight the following key research needs:

(i)   an examination of the extent and nature of
any priority and behavioural changes with regard
to both distributive and integrative bargaining
arrangements and the reasons for such change;
(ii)   an examination of the alleged work and
employment shifts towards the lesser unionised
parts of multi-establishment organisations;
(iii) survey work documenting the extent of introduction of flexible working arrangements;
(iv)   survey work examining the priority management accords to limiting further union recognition,
relative to other industrial relations goals;
(v)   survey work indicating the extent of greenfield site establishments (relative to the growth
of single, independent establishments);
(vi)   further empirical examinations of the management style(s) operative in non-union establishments,
the nature of the union avoidance strategies adopted
and the factors associated with the desire for non-

union status;
(vii) survey work on the extent and nature of
inter-organisation patterns of influence on work
practices and arrangements;
(viii) a systematic examination of the success of
individual union initiatives designed to increase
membership.

        To these priority needs we would add a number
of rather 'lesser' subjects that still warrant
some investigation.   Under this heading we would
include, for example, a study of the factors behind
the relatively successful operation of statutory
recognition provisions in Northern Ireland.   In
addition the value of the recognition findings
revealed by the conciliation data for Scotland
would be enhanced by similar work being undertaken
in other ACAS regions.   As well as the matters
enumerated here it is hoped that some of the
material of previous chapters will have suggested
other topics that individual researchers may wish
to pursue in the future.

Trying to Offset Decline

If the existing incentives for managèment to move
away from union acceptance at the organisational
level increase through time, how can, and should,
unions respond to this situation?   In principle,
the unions can respond in two possible ways: (i)
accept the reality of increased management opposition and try to make gains in the face of it;
and (ii) seek to reduce this opposition by 'changing
their ways'.   There are obvious limits to the
extent to which unions can, and should, change their
ways.   For example, although one might urge
individual unions to identify themselves with the
fortunes of individual companies, the reality of
union structure in the UK clearly prevents a move
towards this sort of 'enterprise unionism' of the
Japanese type; Brown has, however, suggested that
the recession is causing shop stewards to be
increasingly dependent on company (as opposed to
union) resources which may be making for a situation
of de facto enterprise unionism,(6)   although
whether this involves individual stewards identifying with the company (as opposed to the individual
plant) is far from clear.   According to Mills and
Lovell, companies increasingly require from unions
(i) a commitment to competitiveness and (ii) a
responsibility for quality, but these are only seen
as likely to come about if companies meet the union
requirements of (i) employment security for the

membership and (ii) acceptance of a broader leadership role for the unions.(7)   These arrangements
would involve the practices listed below in Table
8.2.

Table 8.2:   Practices for Competitiveness

Unions   - individualised treatment by unions of
                companies in wages or working conditi-
                ons or both
              - concern for competitiveness of a
                particular company
              - flexibility in order to provide
                greater efficiency

Companies   - better relations with the rank and
                file (a union cannot deliver employee
                commitment)
              - participative operational decisions
              - delegation of responsibility and
                sharing information
              - emphasis on employment security
              - compensation system possesses varia-
                bility as business conditions and/or
                performance alters (i.e. competitive-
                ness requires a greater flexibility
                in compensation to reduce employment
                variability).

Source: D. Quinn Mills and Malcolm Lovell,
           'Enhancing Competitiveness: Contribution
           of Employee Relations', in Bruce R. Scott
           and George C. Lodge, U.S. Competitiveness
           in the World Economy, Harvard Business
           School Press, Boston, Mass., 1985,
           p.463.

A similar perspective is adopted in Richard
Walton's recent article on the movement from
control to commitment in the workplace.(8)   A
particularly useful aspect of Walton's work is the
identification of a transitional stage between
control and commitment strategies, which involves
the following features:

(1) Job design principles - scope of individual
                             responsibility extended
                             to upgrading system
                             performance, via
                             participative problem
                             solving groups.

(2) <u>Compensation policies</u> - equality of sacrifice among employee groups.

(3) <u>Employment assurances</u> - assurance that participation will not result in job loss
  - extra efforts to avoid lay-offs.

(4) <u>Employee voice policies</u>
  - addition of limited, ad hoc consultation mechanisms
  - additional sharing of information.

(5) <u>Labour-management relations</u>
  - thawing of adversarial attitudes; joint sponsorship of employee involvement, emphasis on common fate.

These are the major ways in which unions have been urged to change their attitudes and behaviour; it is important to note that these suggestions invariably require a <u>prior</u> change by management (e.g. information sharing), and supportive policies by government (e.g. re-employment programmes for displaced employees.) In addition the seminal work of Freeman and Medoff in the United States reached the following conclusions:(9)

> Should someone who favours, as we do, a thriving market economy, also favour a strong union movement and be concerned with the on-going decline in private sector unionism? According to our research findings, yes.

> Should someone who wants a thriving, profitable company, as managers and stockholders rightly do, oppose the unionisation of his or her firm? According to our research findings, the answer is generally yes. The paradox of American unionism is that it is at one and the same time a plus on the overall social balance sheet (in most though not all circumstances) and a minus on the corporate balance sheet (again, in most though not all circumstances). We believe that this paradox underlies the national ambivalence towards unions. What is good for society at large is not necessarily good for GM (or any other specific company).

Conclusions

Freeman and Medoff then went on to suggest
measures to strengthen the voice/response face of
unionism (along the lines proposed by Mills and
Lovell), weaken the monopoly face (i.e. measures to
increase competitive pressures in the system) and
proposed legislative changes to increase the
organisational capability of the union movement.
In view of the contents of Chapter 3 it is not surprising that we would also urge the need for a
serious re-think of the future role of statutory
recognition provisions in the UK.   This re-think
should involve the positive lessons to be learnt
from experience in both Northern Ireland and Canada.
Admittedly, further, detailed research is required
in both cases, but these two systems appear to have
achieved (with quite different procedures) the
blend or mixture of a relatively high union win
rate, apparently relatively few administrative
problems for the third party decision making body
and little in the way of significant political
opposition and pressure for their repeal from the
employers' side.   A simple transfer of either of
these procedures to Great Britain may be neither
possible nor appropriate, but certainly any future
set of such provisions must give central consideration to the degree of discretion allowed to the
third party decision making body in hearing, and
deciding recognition claims, the length of time
permitted in the hearing and decision making
process and the type of sanction available for
ensuring employer compliance with the third party
recommendations.   The question of whether the
voluntary conciliation route to recognition
should be fully incorporated or integrated into
such statutory provisions also requires consideration.

Legislative (and accompanying administrative)
change may also be necessary to facilitate, as
opposed to simply enable, union growth through the
transfer of engagements and amalgamation route.
The Trade Union Amalgamation Act has now been on
the statute book for more than 20 years, a fact
which suggests that some of its provisions may be
in need of revision in order to more accurately
reflect contemporary circumstances.   And certainly
if the encouragement of internal employee representation bodies becomes an increasingly favoured
tactic of employers pursuing a union substitution
approach then the passage of legislation with a
clearly specified list of criteria for granting
certificates of independence would seem to

constitute something of a union priority.

However, in a union movement which has traditionally emphasised organisation through voluntary
means a major challenge for the future will be to
restrict (as it certainly cannot eliminate) the
degree of inter-union competition for recognition.
This need may require the TUC to produce a code of
practice specifying the minimal terms and conditions
for an acceptable procedural agreement. Although
whether there is sufficient consensus within the
movement to produce a meaningful document on this
subject, and whether it could have any practical
impact (given the potential sanctions for non-
compliance), is far from obvious at the present
time. The TUC might also seek to guide further
organising efforts through its existing industry
committees defining appropriate spheres of influence
and actually orchestrating co-ordinated campaigns.
This has been done to some extent already. The
printing industry committee has sought to do this
in relation to the 'target firm' of D.C. Thompson,
although with little obvious success over an
extended period of time. Considerably more
success apparently attended the Hotel and Catering
Industry Committee's use of a union boycott of
Scarborough as a conference centre to assist the
GMWU obtain recognition agreements with various
individual hotels in the area. This particular
experience was undoubtedly facilitated by the
absence of inter-union competition for recognition,
although its spatial concentration, which permitted
pressure to be brought on various bodies in the
area, could certainly constitute something of a
model for the future.

At the level of the individual trade union
there are two quite different issues or areas of
change that will need to be contemplated. The
first is that if a priority is to be attached to
the organisation of new bargaining units then there
will need to be a move away from the decentralised
personally orientated and generally reactive
approach to organisation in the past. Organisation
will have to become more of a centralised and
specialist activity with detailed attention being
given to questions such as the optimum timing of
organising moves and the identification of firm or
plant specific sources of job dissatisfaction
to aid such organisation. The other issue for
consideration is the extent to which individual
unions are prepared to assume more of an advocate-
advisor role for individual employees. This route

may be the means for reducing non-membership in recognised units and/or gaining a second tier of membership in situations that will be difficult to bring under formal collective bargaining arrangements.

Finally, it is worth returning to Freeman and Medoff's observation that a continuing fall in union density should be of concern to more than simply the trade union movement. A recent paper on the US industrial relations system posed the following 'disturbing questions' for the future:(10)

(i)   Since trade unions have contributed to the stability of democratic societies throughout the West, will labour's decline in the United States unsettle that equilibrium?
(ii)   Will the benign aspects of human resource management continue in the absence of organised labours countervailing power?
(iii)   Will massive lay-offs, plant closings and wage cuts create a backlash if labour market conditions tilt again in favour of employees?

It is difficult to imagine that such questions could ever come to be seriously posed in the UK, although that is probably what a lot of individuals thought in the United States some 20 years ago.

NOTES

1.   T.A. Kochan, R.B. McKersie and P. Cappelli "Strategic Choice and Industrial Relations Theory", Industrial Relations, Vol.23, No.1, Winter 1984, p.26.
2.   Hugh Clegg, Trade Unionism Under Collective Bargaining, Basil Blackwell, Oxford, 1976, pp.68-82.
3.   P.B. Beaumont, A.W.J. Thomson and M.B. Gregory, "Bargaining Structure", Management Decision, Vol.18, No.3, 1980, p.114.
4.   Alan Gladstone and Muncto Ozak, "Trade Union Recognition for Collective Bargaining Purposes", International Labour Review, Vol.CXII, August-September 1975, pp.165-167.
5.   Donna Sockell, "The Legality of Employee-Participation Programs in Unionized Firms", Industrial and Labor Relations Review, Vol.37, No.4, July 1984, pp.541-556.
6.   William Brown, "Britain's Unions: New Pressures and Shifting Loyalties", Personnel Management, October 1983, pp.48-51.

7.   D. Quinn Mills and Malcolm Lovell, "Enhancing Competitiveness: The Contribution of Employee Relations", in Bruce R. Scott and George C. Lodge (eds), US Competitiveness in the World Economy, Harvard Business School Press, Boston, Mass., 1985, p.462.

8.   Richard E. Walton, "From Control to Commitment in the Workplace", Harvard Business Review, March-April 1985, pp.77-84.

9.   R.B. Freeman and J.L. Medoff, What Do Unions Do?, Basic Books, New York, 1984, p.248.

10.   Jack Barbash, "Do We Really Want Labor On The Ropes?", Harvard Business Review, July-August 1985, p.20.

Index

A

ꞁ

6 A

A

-A